STUART DAVIS

Stuart Davis

PATRICIA HILLS

Harry N. Abrams, Inc., Publishers
IN ASSOCIATION WITH
The National Museum of American Art, Smithsonian Institution

Series Director: Margaret L. Kaplan
Editor: James Leggio
Designer: Ellen Nygaard Ford
Photo Research: Neil Ryder Hoos

Library of Congress Cataloging-in-Publication Data

Hills, Patricia.
    Stuart Davis/Patricia Hills.
        p. cm. — (The Library of American Art)
    Includes bibliographical references and index.
    ISBN 0–8109–3219–9 (hardcover)
        1. Davis, Stuart, 1892–1964.   2. Artists—United States—
    Biography.   I. Title.   II. Series: The Library of American Art
    (Harry N. Abrams, Inc.)
N6537.D3345H55   1996
759. 13—dc20
[B]

95–22046

Frontispiece: *Rue Lipp,* page 13

Published in 1996 by Harry N. Abrams, Incorporated, New York
A Times Mirror Company

Printed and bound in Japan

Contents

1. *Self-Portrait*

Acknowledgments

The recent scholarship on Stuart Davis, especially that included in the catalogue for the Stuart Davis retrospective exhibition organized by Lowery Stokes Sims and held at the Metropolitan Museum of Art in 1991, has set a high standard for subsequent scholars. I feel fortunate in having benefitted from the research of the contributors to that catalogue, including William C. Agee, Robert Hunter, Lewis Kachur, Diane Kelder, John R. Lane, and Karen Wilkin. Other scholars and critics whose writings have augmented my knowledge of Davis include Brian O'Doherty, Diane Tepfer, Bruce Weber, and Rebecca Zurier. I am particularly grateful to Lowery Sims for her help in obtaining photographs and for her encouragement.

Scholars of Stuart Davis's art, including myself, have been greatly aided by the help of the artist's son, Earl Davis, who has provided insights into his father's art and has shared many unpublished documents and notes. Without his advice and his contribution to my own research efforts I would not have been able to write the present book.

I also want to thank the following individuals for facilitating my research at their institutions: Garnett McCoy, Cynthia Ott, and Robert Brown at the Archives of American Art, Washington, D.C., and Boston; Theodore E. Stebbins, Jr., and Erica Hirshler at the Museum of Fine Arts, Boston; Lisa McDermott at the Rose Art Gallery, Brandeis University, Waltham, Massachusetts; Britt Crews at the Cape Ann Historical Association, Gloucester, Massachusetts; Barbara Dayer Gallati and Deborah Wythe at the Brooklyn Museum, New York; Judith Zilczer at the Hirshhorn Museum and Sculpture Garden, Smithsonian Institution, Washington, D.C.; Rona Roob, Fiona Howe, and Lisa Archambeau at the Museum of Modern Art, New York; David G. Currie of New Trier High School in Winnetka, Illinois; Elizabeth Hutton Turner at the Phillips Collection, Washington, D.C.; Suzette DuToit, Lawrence B. Salander, and William Edward O'Reilly of the Salander-O'Reilly Galleries, New York; Kate Childs of Sotheby's, New York; Melissa Kronin at the National Museum of American Art, Washington, D.C.; Nancy Roden and Anita Duquette at the Whitney Museum of American Art, New York; Bernadette Cheek of East Orange High School, New Jersey; and Virginia Smith of Gloucester. Boston University graduate students William Moore and Stephanie Taylor helped me track down periodical literature.

During the years when I was engaged in this project, I talked with many people who knew Davis. I especially appreciate the time taken by the following individuals, who shared their memories with me: Helen Sloan, Gene Goosen, Will Barnet, Terry Dintenfass, Jacob Lawrence, Audrey Flack, Naomi Miller, and the late Raphael Soyer. I am also grateful to Wanda Corn and Beth Turner for reading the present book in an early draft form and for offering useful criticisms. As always, thanks to Kevin Whitfield for endlessly listening as I tried to think through the art and persona of Stuart Davis.

Finally, it was a pleasure to work with James Leggio, Neil Ryder Hoos, and Ellen Nygaard Ford at Harry N. Abrams, Inc.

1. *Self-Portrait*

1912. Oil on canvas, 32¼ x 26¼"
Collection Earl Davis, courtesy
Salander-O'Reilly Galleries, New York

Davis's image of himself—an angry young man, dressed like an office clerk, prowling the streets of a working-class district—resembles the protagonist of an early-twentieth-century realistic novel, Theodore Dreiser's young working-class artist in The "Genius" *(1915), who comes to New York and achieves a reputation as an illustrator and advertising art director. The painting qualities of* Self-Portrait *indicate Davis's awareness of European fin-de-siècle moodiness and eccentric composition quite unlike the portraits of his mentors, Robert Henri and John Sloan.*

2. *The Back Room*

Introduction:
The Making of a Hip Modernist

It don't mean a thing, if it ain't got that swing.
> —Duke Ellington (inscribed on Davis's
> *American Painting,* plate 92)

STUART DAVIS LEFT A STRONG IMPRINT ON the history of American art. For six decades he painted, and he argued endlessly with fellow artists, critics, museum people, and, during the 1930s, government bureaucrats. From the 1920s to his death in 1964 he developed a personal art theory in his writings and lectures, scorning academic banality, sentimentality, and bourgeois sensibilities. All along he maintained an experimental outlook toward the making of art. To Davis, art and life were inseparable, and he championed his own kind of modernism as an art with social meaning. Each painting was directed to the public and was intended to stir up ideas and feelings about contemporary experience.

He lambasted anti-urban and antimodern cultural nationalism, epitomized, he thought, by the art of Thomas Hart Benton, but he nevertheless took pains to declare that his own art had its origins in the American experience. He identified with the urban America of everyday working people and with a culture infatuated with technology, consumer goods, and packaging, one that celebrated the small-time entrepreneur and at the same time responded to the rhythms of popular music and jazz.

Davis was raised in an unpretentious, urban, artistic community—too hard-working for bohemia but sharing bohemia's life-styles and easygoing ethos. Both his parents had trained at the Pennsylvania Academy of the Fine Arts, undoubtedly the best art school in America at that time, primarily because it upheld the teaching philosophy of Thomas Eakins—namely, an anti-academic approach to art and an anti-Puritan attitude toward life, coupled with disciplined methods. Davis's mother, Helen Stuart Foulke Davis, a sculptor, exhibited in Philadelphia and New York. His father, Edward Wyatt Davis, earned the family income by working as a newspaper art editor. Edward Davis had high standards; he regularly turned down hack illustrators and instead hired the leading young realists of Philadelphia, such as John Sloan, William Glackens, George Luks, and Everett Shinn. Edward Davis related well to people on the move, to people seeking new ideas and ways of doing things. He himself tinkered with entrepreneurial schemes on the side: one year he started a company

2. *The Back Room*

1913. Oil on canvas, 30¼ x 37½"
Whitney Museum of American Art, New York.
Gift of Mr. and Mrs. Arthur Altschul, 69.114

While the friezelike composition and the paint handling of deep shadows are traditional, the subject of The Back Room *is daring—the darkened interior of a Newark barrel house where music is being played by the Four Leaf Clover band while the patrons dance, drink, and lurch at one another. When newspaperman Emanuel Julius went with Davis in 1915 to such a place, where the patrons were both black and white, he noted that the owner was white. "Later we learned that all those places— saloons, dives, dance halls, vice spots— were owned and run by white men." The cultural influences through ragtime, swing, and jazz from the urban African-American community were to have a lifelong hold on Davis.*

to produce "Gumlax," the original chewing-gum laxative, but could not quite make a go of it.[1] These talented and resourceful parents supported young Davis's interest in the arts from the beginning. After moving to East Orange, New Jersey, they encouraged Stuart to pursue his art training in nearby New York City.[2] Their friends Robert Henri and Sloan were mentors to Stuart and made certain he had exhibition opportunities in New York.

Living on his own, in a studio in Newark and later in New York, Davis was drawn to the bohemian life that centered on Greenwich Village. Besides painting daily, his routine included free lunches at neighborhood saloons, chess games in coffeehouses, midnight beers at jazz cellars, trips to the editorial offices of little magazines, political meetings, and avant-garde artistic activities. Summers saw Davis roaming the art colonies in New England, sketching the scenery and participating in more art talk.

Because Davis flourished in the art world of his parents' friends, he seems never to have felt the need to break with them. Living arrangements and finances were merely practical problems that had to be solved cooperatively; bourgeois notions of decorum, property, and financial self-sufficiency never entered into their considerations. For instance, when he was twenty-two years old, his mother brought his little brother, Wyatt, and joined him in Gloucester where they lodged ("roughed it" might be more accurate) along with other artists—Charles and Alice Beach Winter and John and Dolly Sloan—at the tiny "Red Cottage." Not privacy but the making of art was the primary concern. When Davis went to Paris in the late 1920s, his parents advanced him funds so that he could extend his stay after his money ran out; and it was in letters to them that he poured out his impressions of the expatriate life. At that time his parents were living in the Chelsea Hotel on Twenty-third Street in Manhattan, even then a residence for bohemian literary and artistic types.

In the first two decades of the twentieth century, Greenwich Village became the nerve center of oppositional politics—a politics shaped by the Progressive Era.[3] To artists, being progressive meant arguing against the hypocrisy of Victorian prudery and the snobbery of the wealthy, and bringing America into the technological twentieth century. Freedom, individuality, and justice became rallying cries, as artists lent their skills and time to reformist causes and working-class struggles. Among those in the Davis family's circle of friends, Robert Henri was an anarchist, John Sloan joined the Socialist Party, and Dolly Sloan became a suffragist and worked tirelessly in support of the protracted 1912 strike of mill workers in Lawrence, Massachusetts. The progressive, socialist, and bohemian spirit produced one of the liveliest magazines of the era—The Masses, of which Sloan was the unpaid art director and to which Henri and many of his New York students contributed. Davis cut his teeth as a professional illustrator in his work for The Masses.

Of course, early on he was exposed to the ideas of Henri and Sloan as to what being "American" might mean in an era of progressive reform. To Robert Henri's generation—strongly influenced by the poetry of Walt Whitman—to be "American" meant to capture the spirit of everyday, working-class people, immi-

3. *Studio Interior*

1917. Oil on canvas, 18¾ x 23"
The Metropolitan Museum of Art, New York.
George A. Hearn Fund, 1994

In the late teens Davis looked to the European Post-Impressionists, such as van Gogh, and to Matisse and the Fauves as exemplars of a modern art. Thus, not surprisingly, his Studio Interior *pays homage to both Vincent van Gogh's* Bedroom in Arles *(1888) and Henri Matisse's* The Red Studio *(1911), yet the modern Victrola for playing phonograph records and the typewriter on the desk at the lower right clearly reflect Davis's own interests—listening to music and writing.*

3. *Studio Interior*

4. *Lucky Strike*

1924. Oil on paperboard, 18 x 24″
Hirshhorn Museum and Sculpture Garden,
Smithsonian Institution, Washington, D.C.
Museum Purchase, 1974

During the early and middle 1920s, Davis continued to experiment with different modernist approaches, yet he almost always showed a strong impulse to include the everyday objects of masculine popular culture such as seen here: a newspaper sports page, tobacco, cigarette papers, and a pipe.

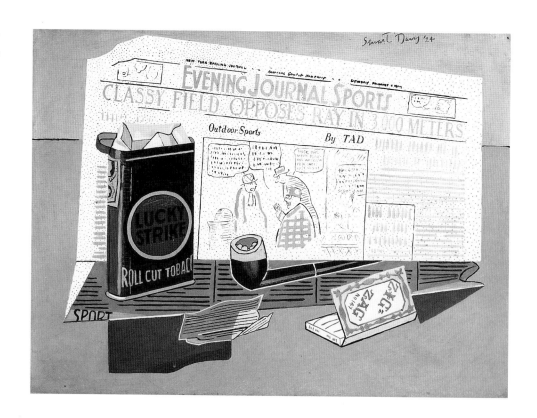

5. *Egg Beater No. 4*

1928. Oil on canvas, 27 x 38⅛″
The Phillips Collection, Washington, D.C.

Urged by critics to forgo his eclectic artistic experiments and settle down, and supported by funds from Mrs. Gertrude Vanderbilt Whitney, Davis spent a year, 1927–28, sequestered in his studio with a table still life consisting of an electric fan, a rubber glove, and an egg beater. His intense concentration on abstracting his compositions from the geometric shapes, planes, and spaces surrounding and penetrating these disparate objects resulted in four major paintings that achieved critical success. In October 1939, Davis hoped for a sale to Duncan Phillips, an early patron of his. He wrote Phillips that Egg Beater No. 4 *"represents the best example of this series which enabled me to realize certain structural principles that I have continued to use ever since. I took this picture to Paris with me and it was admired by Léger."*

6. *Rue Lipp*

1928. Oil on canvas, 32 x 39"
The Crispo Collection

According to Lewis Kachur, this Davis street scene made multiple references to Davis's old friend from the Masses *days, the poet Robert Carlton Brown, then in Paris. The title referred to the Brasserie Lipp, which Davis frequented. The composition of the painting formed the basis of* The Paris Bit *of 1959 (plate 118).*

grants included, who lived in the cities. To foreign visitors and citizens alike, New York seemed particularly "American," with its newly erected skyscrapers, its subways, its theaters and parks, and its many ethnic neighborhoods burgeoning with recently arrived immigrants. One enthusiast was Robert J. Coady, who in 1916–17 published an avant-garde magazine, *The Soil.* This magazine so impressed Davis that he eagerly anticipated each issue and as late as 1962 urged one interviewer to search the library for it.

In the first issue Coady wrote an article called "American Art," primarily a Whitmanesque list of subjects for "young, robust, energetic, naive, immature, daring and big spirited" American art. These subjects included "The Skyscraper and Colonial Architecture. . . . The Bridges, the Docks, the Cutouts, the Viaducts . . . Wright's and Curtiss's Aeroplanes and the Aeronauts. The Sail Boats, the Ore Cars. . . . Rag-time . . . Syncopation and the Cake-walk. The Crazy-Quilt and the Rag-mat . . . Krazy Kat, Tom Powers . . . Walt Whitman and Poe."[4] In 1962, Davis still recalled Coady's daring layout that juxtaposed disparate images: "He'd have a picture of an African structure on one page and the latest locomotive on the next page." To Davis, this "broader thinking about art in the whole community, about art being in technology, machinery and all that" was new and exciting.[5]

The Soil had such a long-lasting influence on Davis because it promoted both a popular and an international "Americanness." For Davis, being American was a question of personal geographical placement and of being open to

7. Interior

1930. Oil on canvas, 24 x 20"
Museum of Fine Arts, Boston.
The William H. Lane Collection

When Davis returned to New York from Paris in 1929 he developed several stylistic variations that moved away from the playful, simplified imagery and perspectival ordering of Parisian building facades. Interior *balances recognizable but highly abstracted forms—such as a chair back missing one vertical piece and an artist's easel against which rests a partially painted canvas—with large areas of empty space, punctuated by straight and calligraphic lines and surrounded by a frame of orange paint.*

8. *House and Street*

1931. Oil on canvas, 26 x 42¼"
Whitney Museum of American Art,
New York. Purchase

House and Street *represents another post-Parisian style. According to Rudi Blesh, the music critic who in 1960 wrote one of the earliest books on the artist, Davis had for some time been working toward the unity of separate views: "Not superimposed but side by side as if they had gotten paired by mistake on an old-fashioned, stereoscopic view card." To Blesh, what was new in* House and Street *was Davis's "shock through dis-location, of the use of the double image as a normal way of seeing, the whole present-day philosophy of the conjunction of disparates."*

the most vital influences of the environment. In 1930, he wrote: "I am as American as any other American painter . . . an American whether I want to be or not. While I admit the foreign influence I strongly deny speaking their language. . . . Over here we are racially English-American, Irish-American, German-American, French, Italian, Russian or Jewish-American and artistically we are Rembrandt-American, Renoir-American and Picasso-American. But since we live here and paint here we are first of all, American."[6] All his life he would argue vehemently against chauvinist definitions of "Americanism."

This milieu of friends and mentors—where current events and political issues were discussed, debated, and acted upon, but where the making of art remained one's primary goal—would shape Davis's subsequent life. In his many letters during the Depression years soliciting patrons and potential patrons to purchase his art, he made it clear that he simply wanted to be able to continue making art without the distraction of other income-producing activities. He never gave a thought to accumulating wealth or even saving money. Studio space and art supplies were his only necessities; liquor, tobacco, and jazz records his only luxuries.

By and large, he moved in a man's world. His buddies were, in the early teens, Glenn Coleman and Henry Glintenkamp; later, during the 1930s, they included John Graham and Arshile Gorky, and then dozens of artists and writers on the political left. In the 1940s and 1950s, he frequented nightspots and became fast friends with the drummer George Wettling and other jazz musicians. Women played a role and could be equals, but the men made the rules. If women socialized with men, it was to join them drinking at jazz spots. Although Davis married twice, his wives rarely figured in his writings, letters, or conversations with interviewers. Not that he was cool to them; he just never took to conventional domesticity. Nor did Davis, unlike a great number of other artists of his generation, acquire a reputation as a womanizer. When I questioned Helen Farr Sloan, John Sloan's widow, if Davis was the sort who had affairs with women, she replied with the succinct comment: "He was a sensualist."[7] She meant that Davis was alive to all sensory experiences. A lengthy, illicit liaison was not his style, for it would have distracted him from his art activities.

Davis's relationships were openly social and collective, not private and personal. In art school, magazine editorial offices, coffeehouses, and saloons of the Village, he developed into a witty raconteur and tough polemicist. He particularly thrived in artists' groups, many of which he organized and led. He had the intelligence and imagination to grasp the necessity of consensus and group effort, a gift for organizing, the tenacity and discipline to stick to a program of action and follow through with details, and the oratorical skills to keep a meeting of disparate people on course. His organizational gifts, like his antibourgeois outlook, appeared early in life. In grammar school he had been selected president of his school class, he later recalled, since "nobody else wanted the job. . . . I had no belly-aches about anything."[8] At times he alienated his opponents, as well as friends, in his passion to energize an organization for the greater good of modern artists. He could be downright scrappy, sparring in print with the American Regionalists Thomas Hart Benton and John Steuart Curry, and he continually fired off letters of terse invective to newspapers and government bureaucrats. The histories of the major radical and progressive American artists' organizations—such as the Artists Union and the American Artists Congress of the 1930s—could hardly be written without acknowledging the central role played by Stuart Davis.

His intensely social nature was matched by his equally intense commitment to documenting his thoughts on the theory and practice of art. His verbal adroitness and theoretical bent are revealed in journals he kept for decades, beginning in the 1920s, concerning the artistic problems he was working through in his art practice. It has been estimated that Davis's theoretical writings exceed ten thousand manuscript pages.[9] Add to these his hundreds of letters, notes on meetings, and drafts of speeches, as well as his published articles, and we have a body of writing unique among twentieth-century American artists. His own theories of composition and color dominate his journal ruminations, along with, in the 1930s, theories about the relationship of art to society and the special relevance modern art had for its era. When we read the endless variations of his developing "space-color" concepts, it becomes clear that such writings were a necessary part of the process of converting theory into practice, into concrete works of art. He also left notebooks filled with drawings of scenes and objects, sketches of compositional problems he was working through, and quick renderings of the paintings of other artists. Daily calendars contain not just notes about appointments but scribbled comments on the progress of specific paintings. In the papers available for study so far, we do not find writings that are personal in subject or tone. There are no romantic confessions, no despondent self-doubts, no musings of a spiritual nature. The man revealed in all these writings is orderly, pragmatic, responsive to his social environment and to the ordinary "man on the street," and committed to action and change.

In spite of his organizational bent, and his facility as an art theorist and political polemicist, Davis will be remembered primarily as a modernist artist. When the first great wave of modernism hit the American public—the "International Exhibition of Modern Art," held at the Sixty-ninth Regiment Armory and known as the Armory Show—he was overwhelmed.[10] The exhibition confirmed some of the experiments he had already made with reducing form to planes and using nonimitative color. It also gave him, he later recalled, a sense of an "objective order" similar to the syncopated rhythms of jazz piano players. He resolved to "become a 'modern' artist."[11]

Indeed, the sources of Davis's modernist experimentation were not limited solely to contact with art-world developments. In the early years the literary intellectuals also inspired him, and thus he was particularly honored when William Carlos Williams sought his permission to reproduce one of his drawings as the frontispiece of Williams's volume of poetry *Kora in Hell: Improvisations* (1920). Davis's association with the literary avant-garde continued into the 1920s; *The Dial* included his drawings in several issues in the early 1920s, and

9. *Shapes of Landscape Space*

c. 1938. Gouache on paper, 13 x 10"
Davison Art Center, Wesleyan University,
Middletown, Connecticut

During the middle to late 1930s, Davis was heavily involved with the daily organizational problems of the Artists Union and the American Artists Congress. Unlike other artists committed to activism, Davis rarely allowed overt political messages to enter his art, either as subject or content. However, in painting abstract compositions inspired by his sketches of the Gloucester waterfront, Davis vigorously maintained the social relevance of such works. As he wrote in his essay "Abstract Painting Today" in 1939: "Abstract painting in its mural, easel, and graphic forms has given concrete artistic formulation to the new lights, speeds, and spaces which are uniquely real in our time." For this reason, "abstract art is a progressive social force."

his expatriate friend Elliot Paul, editor of the journal *transition,* ran an article at the time of Davis's 1928–29 Paris sojourn that promoted the artist as a modern painter of daring independence.

Another source for Davis's modernism was the cultural presence and music of black America, which he came consciously to acknowledge from the 1930s onward. When the art historian Richard Powell singled out artists who had created a "blues aesthetic" in America; he rightly placed Davis in that pantheon of mostly African-American artists.[12] "Influence" hardly serves as a word or concept to describe Davis's artistic evolution, since he absorbed elements of African-American culture from the very beginning of his consciousness of the arts. His father, who came from the South, took young Stuart to what were then

10. *Hot Still-Scape for Six Colors—Seventh Avenue Style*

1940. Oil on canvas, 36 x 47″
Museum of Fine Arts, Boston. Gift of the
William H. Lane Foundation and the M. and M.
Karolik Collection, by exchange, 1983.120

In the early 1940s, Davis began meeting the leading New York jazz musicians and attending all-night jam sessions. Like a jazz soloist who takes a well-known melody and improvises flourishes and variations, Davis learned to riff on his earlier compositions. Thereafter, almost all of his major oils came from compositions worked out in his earlier paintings. Egg Beater No. 2 *(plate 65), with its parallelogram stretching from the upper left to the lower right, formed the basis for* Hot Still-Scape.

Writing in 1940 for Parnassus *magazine, Davis commented on the painting: "It is composed from shape and color elements which I have used in painting landscapes and still-lifes from nature. Invented elements are added. Hence the term 'Still-scape.' It is called 'Hot' because of its dynamic mood, as opposed to a serene or pastoral mood. Six colors, white, yellow, blue, orange, red, and black, were used as the materials of expression. They are used as the instruments in a musical composition might be, where the tone-color variety results from the simultaneous juxtaposition of different instrument groups. It is '7th Ave. Style' because I have had my studio on 7th Ave. for 15 years."*

11. Davis in his studio, 1953

When this photograph was reproduced in Art News *in 1953, its caption read: "Davis at work in his Seventh Avenue studio, New York. An ardent jazz and television fan, he can watch a program of a U.N. debate while preparing his neat palette to begin* Rapt at Rappaport's *on the large canvas." The critic Lawrence Alloway, writing for* The Nation *in February 1978 about the exhibition of Davis's work at the Brooklyn Museum, testified to the power of this photograph: "Stuart Davis made a great impression on me when I lived in England. I saw a photograph of him painting in his studio with the television on; it was the most* American *image of an artist that I had ever seen."*

called "colored shows," such as those put on by Bert Williams and George Walker. The artist recalled that his father "used to sing songs, colored songs. . . . He liked them—I mean he had a sense of humor from the colored standpoint, so I always grew up with that as an automatic thing."[13] Young Davis went to a dancing class at the age of seven and performed on stage as a blackfaced minstrel. At the end of his life he could still remember the lyrics of the ditties he had sung, though now with an ironic consciousness of their racist content.[14] As a youth, Davis became familiar with the black saloons of Newark and Jersey City, particularly enjoying the piano playing. Through these experiences he assimilated the music and culture of ragtime, blues, jazz, and swing, which had originated in black America. White musicians also played a part in this music world. As a gesture of his strong feelings for this culture, he named his only son after two jazz musicians: the white drummer George Wettling and the black piano player Earl Hines.

In the decades of the 1950s and 1960s, Davis's language became increasingly filled with the argot and the wordplay of the "hipster." Jive talk characterizes his notations to himself as he worked through the compositional problems for *Owh! in San Pao* (plate 12). As noted by the art historian Lowery Sims, Davis had originally called the painting "Motel." His jotted instructions to himself on daily calendar pages between Sunday, August 26, and Labor Day, September 3, 1951, chart the progress of the painting:

August 27 :
Put the
Shift in
reverse on
Motel
Mon, watch
the Gravel
flee.

August 28:
Went into
4th speed
on the
Motel Stutz
It has Pants
in its Ants
but—Look Out.

August 30:
The Motel Stutz
turned into
a Lincoln like
a Real Gone
Icon.

August 31:
Motel Lincoln
given a real
Shake Down
Cruise. Has
a cough in its
exhaust
Bought Gas
Mask for
tomorrow.

September 1:
Finished Color—
Shape Content of
Motel at Export Level
Name changed to
"Owh! in San Pao"
Needs 2 days drying
for final execution
of all colors sans Turps.

September 3:
The Motel Lincoln
turned into a
Cadillac
Owh! in San Pao.
Let it Dry Mac,
then Scrape
and Package.
Labor Day
is right.[15]

This was more than just hipster talk. We can now recognize that the rhymes, puns, wordplay, metaphors, and hyperbole that Davis used in his slang description of his painting process relate to one of the modes of black English—specifically a style of speech performance within the African-American community in which typically men, but sometimes women, strive to outperform each other through wit and exaggeration.[16] One can easily imagine Davis speaking such argot in the company of his musician friends.

As Davis explained to radio interviewer John Wingate in 1957, he knew all about hip from the jazz parlors of his youth long before being "hip" was fashionable. When queried about the distinguishing characteristics of "the very hip people," Davis replied that they were "the people competent and able—and have demonstrated in various ways—to know what other people are talking about." He described the un-hip as "those who don't pay attention."[17] To Davis, "hip" characterized what it meant to take the totality of his experiences as an artist and as an American and to make a modern, disciplined art that spoke to the people on the city streets.[18]

Following pages:

12. *Owh! in San Pao*

1951. Oil on canvas, 52¼ x 41¾"
Whitney Museum of American Art, New York.
Purchase, 52.2

Davis based the composition of Owh! in San Pao *on* Percolator *of 1927 (plate 62), but whereas the earlier painting has subdued color, and is centripetally unified with small shardlike planes, the later painting is more complex, with a hot orange, pink-magenta, bright kelly green, yellow, two bright blues, and black. The "6" remains from the earlier* Percolator *but other calligraphic forms are added along with a plane of orange dots and other rectangles floating off to the sides.*

When told that he had misspelled the name of the Brazilian city São Paulo, the artist responded that it was a painting, "not a geography lesson." For a University of Illinois exhibition catalogue in 1952, he wrote about Owh! *in the jive argot he developed for official comments on his work: "The title of my painting is reasonable in the same way as the image itself. It has been scientifically established that the acoustics of Idealism give off the Humanistic Sounds of Snoring, whereas Reality always says 'Ouch!' Clearly then, when the realism has San Pao as its locale, a proper regard for the protocol of alliteration changes it to 'Owh!'"*

13. *Blips and Ifs*

1963–64. Oil on canvas, 71⅛ x 53⅛"
Amon Carter Museum, Fort Worth.
Acquisition in memory of John de
Menil, Amon Carter Museum,
1961–1966 (1967.195)

12. *Owh! in San Pao*

13. *Blips and Ifs*

14. *Consumers Coal Co.*

I. The Apprentice Years: 1909–1920

THE ART THING WAS ALWAYS PRESENT," Stuart Davis said matter-of-factly to an interviewer two years before his death.[1] Indeed, his birth on December 7, 1892, to two Philadelphia artists made an artistic career inevitable. His father, Edward Wyatt Davis, as art editor of the *Philadelphia Press*, numbered among his friends the dynamic realist artist and teacher Robert Henri. During the late 1890s, before the days of photomechanical reproduction, Edward Davis employed Henri's protégés, the Philadelphia artist-reporters John Sloan, William Glackens, George Luks, and Everett Shinn, to make drawings for his newspaper. Young Stuart's mother, Helen Stuart Foulke Davis, was a sculptor who exhibited regularly at the annual exhibitions of the Pennsylvania Academy of the Fine Arts and at the Philadelphia Museum of Art. Even after the Davis family moved in 1901 to East Orange, New Jersey, where Edward Davis worked as art editor and cartoonist at the *Newark Evening News,* they maintained their ties to their artist friends, who one by one were migrating to New York.[2]

The siren call of the Henri group was so strong for young Stuart that in the fall of 1909, with his parents' blessing, he did not register at East Orange High School but went to study at Henri's school at 1947 Broadway in Manhattan.[3] There Davis received not only art training but a radical point of view, which for Henri combined political anarchism with strong doses of Walt Whitman. To his students Henri extolled freedom of expression—freedom from academic rules, from classical notions of beauty, and from Victorian subject matter, such as virginal womanhood, pastoral landscapes, and picturesque holiday spectacles. These realists wanted to capture the spirit of the working classes and the recent immigrants then changing the cultural landscape of New York City.

When they agreed to let their sixteen-year-old son study with Henri, the Davises were well aware of the reputation that their realist painter friends had developed. The year before, in February 1908, Henri and Sloan had organized an exhibition at the Macbeth Gallery that included their work along with that of their realist friends Glackens, Shinn, and Luks and the independents Maurice Prendergast, Arthur B. Davies, and Ernest Lawson. "The Eight," as they were called, publicized themselves and their anti-academic·pictures, and the press responded with a string of reviews, both enthusiastic and hostile. What brought in the crowds were such epithets as "that black revolutionary gang."[4]

Davis's enthusiasm for Henri's school was immediate. He wrote to his cousin Hazel Foulke on December 3, 1909: "Henri's is different than any other school in the world, and if he should stop I would never go to any other teacher because the rest of them don't know what *real* drawing is, an' that's straight."[5]

14. *Consumers Coal Co.*

1912. Oil on canvas, 29½ x 37½"
Sunrise Museums, Charleston, West Virginia.
Gift of Amherst Coal Co.

Davis's early landscapes in oil show a clear debt to Robert Henri's painterly urban naturalism.

Much later, in 1945, Davis summed up his training in an autobiographical essay. His remarks deserve to be quoted at length, because Davis continued throughout his career to think about art in the terms that Henri had promulgated:

The Henri School was regarded as radical and revolutionary in its methods, and it was. All the usual art school routine was repudiated. Individuality of expression was the keynote, and Henri's broad point of view in his criticisms was very effective in evoking it. Art was not a matter of rules and techniques, or the search for an absolute ideal of beauty. It was the expression of ideas and emotions about the life of the time. We drew and painted from the nude model. The idea was to avoid mere factual statement and find ways to get down some of the qualities of memory and imagination involved in the perception of it. We were encouraged to make sketches of everyday life in the streets, the theater, the restaurant, and everywhere else. These were transformed into paintings in the school studios. On Saturday mornings they were all hung on the wall at the Composition Class. Henri talked about them, about music, literature, and life in general, in a very stimulating manner, and his lectures constituted a liberal education.[6]

Even though Henri's paintings exhibit a casual and bravura brushwork, he valued the discipline of technique. He introduced his students to a range of methods: Hardesty Maratta's system of color gradations, Jay Hambidge's theories of "dynamic symmetry," and Denman Ross's principles of design.[7]

Shortly after Davis joined classes at the school, Henri met with friends, including Sloan, Luks, Shinn, Jerome Myers, and Walter Pach, in January 1910 to organize an extensive exhibition of artists independent of the National Academy of Design. Recalling the success of The Eight in 1908, they hoped to broaden the contributors to include all artists who were regularly rejected by the Academy. The core of organizers—Henri, Sloan, Walt Kuhn, and Rockwell Kent—secured gallery space at 29–31 West Thirty-fifth Street in Manhattan, and the "Exhibition of Independent Artists" opened in April 1910. Of the 103 painters and sculptors represented, a number came from Henri's classes. The organizers invited Davis to send five oil paintings: *Gleam on the Lake* (plate 15), *The Passaic, Ice on the Canal, Sunlight and Steam,* and *Music Hall.* His close friends from the school, Glenn Coleman and Henry Glintenkamp, both about five years his senior, also showed in the exhibition, as well as George Bellows, whose *Club Night* (later called *Both Members of This Club,* 1909; Cleveland Museum of Art) shocked a public accustomed to admiring an art of genteel ladies in white dresses.[8] Davis could claim good company for his professional debut.

Henri urged his students to go out into the streets and experience the neighborhoods of New York. The three buddies, Davis, Coleman, and Glintenkamp, tramped all over Lower Manhattan, Newark, and Hoboken in search of urban sights and experiences that could be worked up into interesting paintings. All three port cities were familiar to Davis; his parents had moved in 1910 to Newark, where Davis himself lived independent of them on James Street, and, in 1912, when he left Henri's school, he rented a studio with Glintenkamp in the Terminal Building on Hudson Street in Hoboken.

15. *Gleam on the Lake*

1910. Oil on canvas, 8 x 10¼"
Collection Earl Davis, courtesy
Salander-O'Reilley Galleries, New York

Shortly after Davis joined Robert Henri's classes in New York, he was invited to submit paintings to the "Exhibition of Independent Artists," held in April 1910 at 29–31 West Thirty-fifth Street in New York. This large exhibition, with almost five hundred works of art, including this painting, sought to show work by Americans often excluded by the conservative but powerful arbiter of taste, the National Academy of Design. In retrospect, the Independents' show can be seen as a precursor for the 1913 Armory Show.

THE APPRENTICE YEARS

15. *Gleam on the Lake*

Some of the favored haunts mentioned by Davis in his 1945 autobiography include Chinatown, the Bowery, the burlesque shows, the Brooklyn Bridge, McSorley's Saloon, the music halls in Hoboken, and the black saloons. While the older Henri gang frequented some of these places, the black saloons appealed especially to Davis's generation. In 1945, at a time when Davis quite explicitly connected his paintings to jazz, the Hoboken and Newark black music scene remained vivid in his memory:

Coleman and I were particularly hep to the jive, for that period, and spent much time listening to the Negro piano players in Newark dives. About the only thing then available on phonograph records was the Anvil Chorus. Our musical souls craved something a bit more on the solid side and it was necessary to go to the source to dig it. These saloons catered to the poorest Negroes, and outside of beer, a favorite drink was a glass of gin with a cherry in it which sold for five cents. The pianists were unpaid, playing for love of art alone. In one place the piano was covered on top and sides with barbed wire to discourage lounging and leaning on it, and give the performer more scope while at work. But the big point with us was that in all of these places you could hear the blues, or tin-pan alley tunes turned into real music, for the cost of a five cent beer.[9]

Hanging out at jazz spots would become a lifelong passion.

Davis's early oil paintings reveal a young painter coming to terms with his training, his eye, and the influences of current art. *Consumers Coal Co.* of 1912 (plate 14) and *Gleam on the Lake* of 1910 (plate 15) clearly show Henri's influence in the way Davis emphasizes the tonal qualities of color and handles the medium broadly. But in his figurative paintings, such as *Self-Portrait* of 1912 (plate 1) and *The Back Room* of 1913 (plate 2), other influences insinuate themselves into his work. Davis was gravitating toward images of a rough bohemia that extended Henri's vocabulary of subjects.

Davis's distinct individuality as an artist emerges with a series of watercolors of 1912–13 done in the environs of his Hoboken studio. Some show men congregating in poolrooms, actors performing on vaudeville stages, or women clowning around with their friends. Others are city scenes with genre elements, typically one to three figures set against a streetlight, a fire escape, or an iron fence, with a cat or two to balance the composition. In a third group of interior scenes a narrative element intrudes, reminiscent of the etchings of Sloan, or the British painter Walter Sickert, or even some of the illustrations in contemporary magazines. In these watercolors Davis represents the demimonde that figures in the stories of naturalist fiction writers such as Stephen Crane and Theodore Dreiser—the struggling shop girls and ambitious clerks cohabiting in dingy furnished rooms.

Davis lent five of these watercolors to the ground-breaking Armory Show— the "International Exhibition of Modern Art," held at the Sixty-ninth Regiment Armory in New York in February and March 1913. The show introduced the American public to European and American developments in contemporary art. While Davis's small watercolors may have been overwhelmed by the nearly

1,300 European and American paintings and sculpture that comprised the show, it was a signal honor to have been asked to participate by Henri's pals Walt Kuhn and Arthur B. Davies.[10]

The exhibition set the critics buzzing, not always favorably. The academic artist Kenyon Cox wrote negatively about the show in *Harper's Weekly:* "This thing is not amusing; it is heartrending and sickening."[11] Theodore Roosevelt gave it a mixed review in *The Outlook:* "There was not a touch of simpering, self-satisfied conventionality anywhere in the exhibition," although "the lunatic fringe was fully in evidence, especially in the rooms devoted to the Cubists and the Futurists, or Near-Impressionists."[12] Despite the opposition, the Armory Show achieved an overwhelming success. There was, however, a larger context to the show. The Chicago lawyer and art collector Arthur Jerome Eddy bought from the exhibition and shortly thereafter wrote a book, *Cubists and Post-Impressionism,* that sang the praises of the new art. To Eddy, the Armory Show had to be understood against the background of radical new ideas "constantly breaking out in unexpected places and while they may seem to be different ideas when expressed in music, painting, sculpture, poetry, architecture, from those expressed in science, religion, politics, social reform, and business generally, they are not; they are all fundamentally the same, namely, they are the ideas of a progress so rapid and radical it may be revolutionary and in a measure destructive."[13] In short, the exhibition fell into step with Progressive Era ideals.

Davis later recalled that the experience of seeing the Armory Show gave him the determination to join the new movement:

I was enormously excited by the show, and responded particularly to Gauguin, Van Gogh, and Matisse, because broad generalization of form and the non-imitative use of color were already practices within my own experience. I also sensed an objective order in these works which I felt was lacking in my own. It gave me the same kind of excitement I got from the numerical precisions of the Negro piano players in the Negro saloons, and I resolved that I would quite definitely have to become a "modern" artist.[14]

Situating the impact of modernist painting within a context of innovative African-American music was certainly characteristic of Davis in 1945, but it could well have been an accurate memory of his actual 1913 thoughts. While dealers on the New York scene in those earlier years, such as Alfred Stieglitz and Marius de Zayas, showed African tribal art in their galleries, and de Zayas even advanced the theory that modern art owed its genesis to the impact of African art on the imaginations of contemporary European artists,[15] Davis was one of the first artists to see the equally modernist spirit in ragtime and other music from the African-American community.

Another cause that engaged the older realists and their ex-students was the reorganization of the socialist magazine *The Masses* in December 1912. The first issue of the magazine had appeared in January 1911, edited by a Dutch émigré, Piet Vlag, with the backing of Rufus Weeks, a wealthy insurance executive and an ardent Socialist Party member. The magazine slowly lost circulation until it

16. *Babe La Tour*

17. *The Doctor*

1912. Watercolor and graphite on
wove paper, 11 x 15"
Elvehjem Museum of Art, University of
Wisconsin-Madison. Gift of D. Frederick Baker
from the Baker/Pisano Collection, 1984.94

Servant Girls *(plate 18) and* The Doctor *were among the five watercolors that Davis sent to the Armory Show in 1913. The others were vaudeville and music hall scenes:* Dance, Babe La Tour, *and* The Musicians. *The title* The Doctor *would seem to indicate that the "doctor" has just concluded his medical examination; however, his scowling face and the woman's gesture suggest an illicit liaison. Davis was quite capable of weaving mystery into his watercolors; another, also dated 1912, is called* Murder on the Estate *(collection Earl Davis) and depicts a dead man sprawled on the ground outside a country manor.*

ceased publication altogether in August 1912. Cartoonist Art Young called an emergency meeting; Dolly and John Sloan, Charles and Alice Beach Winter, and Glenn Coleman joined in and decided to revive the magazine by combining social comment and humor. They invited Max Eastman, a poet and former doctoral student of John Dewey's, to edit the magazine without pay. Dolly Sloan was designated office manager. Since the magazine disdained advertisements, no one ever got paid. The journalist John Reed, later a firsthand witness to the 1917 Russian Revolution, drew up a manifesto that was published beneath the masthead. It read in part: "We intend to be arrogant, impertinent, in bad taste, but not vulgar. We will be bound by no one creed or theory of social reform, but will express them all, provided they be radical. We shall keep up a running destructive and satiric comment upon the month's news. Poems, stories and drawings rejected by the capitalist press on account of their excellence will find a welcome in this magazine; and we hope some day even to be able to pay for them."[16] In 1913, bohemianism mixed very well with social protest.

As John Sloan's protégé, Davis was soon brought in, just as he had been when the older realists organized such ground-breaking exhibitions as the Armory Show. He found the magazine staff a lively bunch of artists and writers who would argue over the contents of each issue and vote on what to include. In those days, to be "modern" also meant to be radical, and *The Masses* proved to be a good place for Davis to try out new ideas and art styles. While many of Davis's drawings continue the angular and exaggerated figural style of his earlier watercolors, he could also work in the very naturalistic style of Sloan, or one that mimicked the swelling lines and flat black-and-white contrasts of Art Nouveau.

16. *Babe La Tour*

1913. Watercolor and pencil on paper, 15 x 11"
National Museum of American Art,
Smithsonian Institution, Washington, D.C.
Gift of Henry M. Ploch

Cabaret scenes were popular among the New York artists in Robert Henri's circle, and Davis infused these watercolors with considerable humor.

18. *Servant Girls*

1913. Watercolor on paper, 15 x 11"
Munson-Williams-Proctor Institute,
Museum of Art, Utica, New York

Davis shows a clear debt to John Sloan in his paintings and watercolors of women engaged in domestic activities together. But whereas Sloan's Sunday, Women Drying Their Hair *(plate 19) emphasizes their camaraderie by representing the young women looking at each other as if engaged in conversation, Davis's women, as in* Servant Girls, *typically look and gesture in opposite directions and seem about to take pratfalls out of the picture frame.*

Davis made an indelible impression on the rest of the staff when he submitted a drawing for the June 1913 issue of two women, wearing hats and chatting with each other (plate 20); one says, "Gee, Mag. Think of us bein' on a magazine cover." Earlier, in its March 1913 issue, *The Masses* had published Davis's drawing of two society ladies (or women with pretensions to society) at the Metropolitan Museum pausing before a sign directing visitors to the Morgan Collection (plate 21). The figures in the two images have a similar compositional relationship; standing close, the one facing forward listens to her

19. John Sloan. *Sunday, Women Drying Their Hair*

1912. Oil on canvas, 25½ x 31½"
Addison Gallery of American Art,
Phillips Academy, Andover, Massachusetts

companion, shown in profile, who makes the inane remark, "Oh I think Mr. Morgan paints awfully well, don't you?" Artists, and the editors who wrote the captions for *The Masses*, lost no opportunity to point out the parasitic nature and cultural vapidity of upper-class women, whereas working-class women were portrayed as bright and lively, even if not conventionally pretty. Although it was published, Davis's *Gee, Mag* cover shocked even the *Masses* staff, many of whom, in spite of their professed radicalism, thought the unflattering depiction of the women too stark and sought to veto the drawing's use.

Some of Davis's crayon drawings inspired by his soirées at the black dance halls and beer saloons (or "barrel houses") in New Jersey were published in *The Masses* from 1913 through 1915. Such drawings might have sparked the interest of newspaper reporter Emanuel Julius, who persuaded Davis and Coleman to take him out on the town. Writing an article on "Night Life in Newark" for the May 30, 1915, issue of the *New York Sunday Call Magazine,* Julius relied on the savvy of Davis and Coleman to guide him through the barrel houses and saloons where Davis himself was picking up the argot of urban black America.[17] To Julius, Davis was "a young artist who enjoys above all to picture the lives of Negroes—their humor, their pathos, their high spots. And Newark is the town where he does his wandering, gathering the impressions that are later used in his extraordinary pictures." Later, in 1918, Davis sketched the famous ragtime composer Scott Joplin at the piano, and one can readily surmise that Joplin himself was the piano player of Davis's 1945 memory—the one who exhibited

21. *At the Metropolitan Museum of Art: "Oh I Think Mr. Morgan Paints Awfully Well, Don't You?"*

1913. Published in *The Masses* 4 (March 1913), p. 15. Collection Earl Davis

20. *"Gee, Mag"*

1913. Cover of *The Masses* 4 (June 1913)

Max Eastman, in his Enjoyment of Living, *recalls the circumstances surrounding the decision to publish Davis's drawing on the cover of the June 1913 issue of* The Masses: *"I can see Sloan at a Masses meeting, holding up a drawing by Stuart Davis of two sad, homely girls from the slums of Hoboken, and proposing the title: 'Gee, Mag, think of us bein' on a magazine cover!' That formed our June [1913] cover, which was much commented upon. It was realism; it was also revolt."*

"numerical precisions" and set the standard of excitement by which Davis could measure the impact of the Armory Show.[18]

Davis's career was going well in 1913. While *The Masses* did not pay its artists and writers, he managed to get hired by Norman Hapgood, who had taken over the editorship of *Harper's Weekly* and sought to emulate the quality of pictures and layout of *The Masses*.[19] The 50-dollar-a-week income allowed Davis to vacation that summer in Provincetown, a fishing town at the tip of Cape Cod that attracted New York artists and writers. In his 1945 autobiography he wrote with characteristic humor of his introduction to the Cape:

1915. Published in *The Masses* 6 (July 1915), p. 10. Collection Earl Davis

23. *Barrel House—Newark*

1913. Published in *The Masses* 5 (February 1914), p. 20. Collection Earl Davis

This drawing relates to the painting The Back Room *(plate 2). Both include a piano player and a set of drums, with barrels lined up against a wall and figures crowding the composition. The drawing more clearly foretells Davis's future style, with a push and pull between the two-dimensional design and the illusion of three-dimensional depth. The clarity of the drawing, the sharp silhouettes, and the linear connections between foreground and background make for a lively scene.*

When the drawing was published in the February 1914 issue of The Masses, *its caption read: "Life's Done Been Gettin' Monotonous Since Dey Bu'ned Down Ou'Ah Church." Given Davis's total immersion in the music of these saloons, one suspects that the irrelevant caption was added by an editor. The drawing can stand alone, a point that was argued by Glenn Coleman, Maurice Becker, and Davis himself when they confronted the editor Max Eastman over the issue of captions.*

Provincetown was a new experience for me, and made me a continuing addict of the New England coast. On arrival I hired a room and a dory. My desire was to get into this boat and row around a lot all over the place. I did, and at nightfall tied it up close to a piling where it floated on the same level with a wharf next to my room. Unfamiliar with the local habit of the sea, I was amazed next morning to find it hanging perpendicularly from its mooring. The water had disappeared, a large expanse of sand flats had taken its place. Ten foot tides were out of my experience, but adjacent townsmen thought the incident very funny. At that time, Provincetown still retained a considerable vestige of its sea-faring past. On clear days the air and water had a brilliance of light greater than I had ever seen, and while this tended to destroy local color, it stimulated the desire to invent high intensity color-intervals.[20]

Paintings done in 1913 and 1914 inspired by his experiences there, such as *Ebb Tide—Provincetown* (plate 24) and *A River View* (plate 25), a Hoboken scene, are bold in design and color. And while they may evoke the northern, Expressionist scenes of Edvard Munch, they show Davis leaving convention behind and moving toward new sources for his experimentation.

The topography, light, and sea were not the only attractions of Provincetown, and Davis admitted that "the presence of artists and writers . . . added intellectual stimulus" to the place.[21] One writer Davis remembered was Norman Hapgood's brother, the writer Hutchins Hapgood,[22] who, with John Sloan, John Reed, Mabel Dodge, and others, organized the 1913 Paterson Strike Pageant and later founded the Provincetown Players with others in the *Masses* crowd. When Davis returned to the Cape in the summer of 1914, he lived in a boardinghouse run by Polly Holliday, the proprietor of the Greenwich Village Inn in New York, where the *Masses* staff liked to congregate. Holliday even gave him a small show in her Provincetown restaurant.[23] Another boarder that year was Charles Demuth, a sophisticated writer and artist, a close friend of the poet William Carlos Williams, and a devotee of cabaret life in Europe. Davis admired Demuth, nine years his senior, and said that "his superior knowledge of what it was all about was a great help" to him.[24] The influence might have gone two ways, for Davis's watercolors of cabaret and vaudeville acts preceded those Demuth was to do in 1916.

In September 1913, Davis and Glintenkamp shut their New Jersey studio and moved to Manhattan, where they rented space in the Lincoln Arcade, at 1931 Broadway, along with Glenn Coleman. They immersed themselves in the New York art world and participated in several exhibitions. Whether he received praise or snickers for his bold experiments, Davis's name began to appear in the news—at times, one suspects, through his own efforts. None other than the noted critic of the *New York Sun,* Henry McBride, made complimentary remarks about the "wicked Stuart Davis" in January 1914, after the artist was included in an exhibition at the MacDowell Club: "We think he has great 'talent.' Two of the studies give you the baffling sense that they are screening something awful. His third 'study' is an innocent arrangement of the flow of a tide creek over the sands, but even in it there are two kinds of water, pale blue and pitch black."[25] (The last work would have been one of Davis's Provincetown studies of the tidal flats.) When Charles Caffin, usually an astute commentator on American artists, wrote for the *New York American* a year later, he was less favorable: "Does Davis really believe that art is only or even mostly a monkey shine of technique?"[26] Typically, both critics gave Davis disproportionate space compared to other exhibiting artists.

In the years 1914–16, while war raged in Europe, the older writers and artists of *The Masses,* such as Max Eastman, Art Young, and John Sloan, took a strong antiwar position—not because they were pacifists who deplored violence, but because, as socialists, they believed that modern wars are created by bosses grabbing for international profits. In contrast to these older men committed to a cause, young Davis had a different agenda. He wanted to make art

24. *Ebb Tide—Provincetown*

1913. Oil on canvas, 38 x 30"
Collection Earl Davis, courtesy Salander-O'Reilly
Galleries, New York

and he, along with Glintenkamp and Coleman, began to resent the extended captions Max Eastman added to their nonpolitical cartoons. Davis enlisted Sloan's support, and at a meeting called in April 1916, they confronted Eastman. Eastman and Art Young justified the captions and reasoned that antiwar propaganda was needed more than ever. The story was carried in the newspapers, and Art Young issued a statement that he did not care for drawings that merely showed "ash cans and girls hitching up their skirts in Horatio Street—regardless of ideas—and without title." The upshot was that Sloan, Davis, Coleman, Maurice Becker, Alice and Charles Winter, and the poet Robert Carlton Brown resigned from the staff.[27]

The separation was most painful to Sloan, who had been a Socialist Party comrade with the other staff members. Davis, on the other hand, was not committed to any line or party program. He could thus, with no qualms or regrets, turn his attention to his art and the lessons he had learned from the Armory

25. *A River View*

26. Davis and friends at Gloucester, summer 1915. Photograph by Charles Allen Winter

Standing in front of the Red Cottage at East Gloucester in 1915 are, from left to right: Dolly Sloan, F. Carl Smith, and John Sloan; seated on the steps: Stuart Davis, Paul Cornoyer, Agnes M. Richmond; standing on the porch: Alice Beach Winter, Katherine Groschke, and Paul Tietjens. Dolly Sloan, a gregarious and tireless worker for social causes, was active in socialist and suffragist affairs. Davis, Sloan, and the Winters all contributed to The Masses.

Show. Years later Max Eastman would uncharitably refer to Davis as "the most unbrotherly-hearted, unclass-conscious, arch-Bohemian, modernistical art-rebel" of the lot.[28] Davis, however, did not disappear from the circle of *Masses* contributors. When the staff was invited to a wealthy patron's home in Philadelphia in February 1917, he went along,[29] and he attended the famous sedition trial brought by the U.S. government against the *Masses* staff held in April 1918.[30]

Art, not politics, certainly dominated his time during the summer months. Dolly and John Sloan located a summer place for the *Masses* artists in Gloucester, Massachusetts, in 1914. Gloucester had long attracted artists with its picturesque views, clear light, and sea breezes, especially when days and nights in humid, hot cities rendered concentrating on art making all but impossible. The landscape painter Fitz Hugh Lane had lived there all year round in the midnineteenth century. In the 1870s, William Morris Hunt had a studio there and the landscape painter William Trost Richards visited. Winslow Homer and Frank Duveneck also summered there at the end of the century.[31] Gloucester provided many potential subjects for artists: the inlets and coves; the rocky shoreline, with Ten Pound Island plunked into the middle of the harbor; the lighthouses; the town itself, with the bulky towers of Our Lady of Good Voyage Catholic Church and the pseudo-Wren spire of the Loring B. Haskell House; the glacier rocks of Dogtown; the meandering roads leading to Rockport at the tip of Cape Ann; the schooners, sloops, and dories; and the fishermen.

A colony of artists soon formed in the mid-teens with the Sloans at its hub. Dolly entertained and John, a natural mentor, began conducting art classes for younger artists. He incorporated into his teaching the color scales of Hardesty G. Maratta, an artist who had turned paint manufacturer. Sloan's own production of canvases during those summers became legend, for once his duties as

25. *A River View*

1913. Oil on canvas, 30 x 37"
Rose Art Museum, Brandeis University,
Waltham, Massachusetts. Gift of Samuel Tonkin,
Rego Park, New York

27. *Gloucester Backyard*

c. 1916. Oil on canvas, 30¼ x 24¼"
Private collection

art editor of *The Masses* were behind him his painting activity accelerated.

In their second summer in Gloucester in 1915, the Sloans urged Davis to visit. Davis recalled his initial reaction: "It had the brilliant light of Province-town, but with the important additions of topographical severity and the architectural beauties of the Gloucester schooner."[32] He stayed in the tiny, one-and-a-half-story Red Cottage, which Dolly and John Sloan had rented in East Gloucester, along with his mother, Helen Stuart Davis; his nine-year-old brother, Wyatt; and Alice and Charles Winter.[33] Each summer from 1915 through 1918, when the Sloans stopped going to Gloucester, Davis made return visits to the Red Cottage. During subsequent years, he stayed in houses rented by other artist couples in East Gloucester, including Theresa Bernstein and William Meyerowitz, until the mid-1920s, when his parents bought a place at 51 Mount Pleasant Avenue, a small road that wound up the hill above the Red Cottage.

Painting by Sloan's side brought Davis into close contact with Maratta's color system, promoted by its inventor as a precise ordering of colors based on the spectrum. Maratta manufactured his colors so that the three primaries (red, yellow, and blue) and three secondaries (orange, green, and purple) were equal in their intervals, unlike traditional artists' colors. He also manufactured six other "hues"—the six colors grayed. When an artist mixed one part of one color to one part of an adjoining color (for example, red and orange to produce red-orange) the newly created color would, in turn, be at the midpoint between red and orange. Maratta likened the system to the twelve keys on the piano, with red as middle C, red-orange as C-sharp, orange as D, and so on. To those unfamiliar with music, he used the analogy of the clock, with each of the twelve colors situated at the numeral of an hour. With the system, artists could create palettes of a "dominating color." Maratta's brochure explained: "To each of the six COL-ORS add a certain amount of the COLOR that is to dominate and to the six HUES add the HUE of this dominating color. Then proceed to paint, using the Palette as though it were 'normal.'" Painters could also create "triads" by establishing three of the twelve colors as dominants on their palette, and using their opposites as secondaries. Not unlike the efficiency movement (Taylorism) then revolutionizing industry, Maratta's system was meant to speed artistic production. An artist "may use the time and energy thus gained to a more free and speedy expression of his ideas. A PALETTE being an instrument, or tool, should be a good one." It is estimated that Sloan, for one, produced ninety paintings in a two-month period by using the system.[34] His enthusiasm was such that he and others planned to expand Maratta's four-page brochure into a longer manual.

What distinguishes the paintings produced with Maratta's paints and theories is a palette of such distinctive hues as cobalt blue, violet, and tomato orange, with corresponding tints and shades—colors not characteristic of the traditional artist's palette. According to the theory, and as long as Maratta colors were used, color harmonies would result whether the hues were tinted or darkened. However, the harmonious compositions produced by the Maratta system often have colors of such equal values (i.e., the degree of black in a color) that they look dull in black-and-white reproductions even when spectacular in color.

28. *Gloucester Terraces*

1916. Crayon and ink on paper, 19 x 15"
Collection Earl Davis, courtesy Salander-O'Reilly
Galleries, New York

This drawing was selected by William
Carlos Williams as the frontispiece for
his volume of poetry Kora in Hell:
Improvisations.

Sloan's paintings from the Gloucester years glow with those violet tones, as do many of Davis's abstract experiments, such as *Sketch—Church Tower* of about 1916 (collection Earl Davis) and the more literal landscapes, such as *Gloucester Landscape (Backyard View)* of 1916 (plate 29).

During his summers in Gloucester in the mid-teens, Davis experimented with more than just color; he also turned to problems of composition, paint application, and repeating motifs. He even took on photography, but photography's premise of light as the organizing principle of composition had no interest to him.[35] The paintings that survive from these years swing along a continuum from the expressive naturalism of crowded, all-over compositions such as *Gloucester Landscape (Backyard View)* to the coloristic freedom of *Gloucester Terraces* (plate 30) to the montage of overlapping pictorial vignettes of the crayon-

29. *Gloucester Landscape (Backyard View)*

1916. Oil on canvas, 23⅞ x 29⅜"
Private collection, courtesy Salander-O'Reilly
Galleries, New York

Davis spent his summers in the section of Gloucester called East Gloucester. Like Gloucester itself, the area consists of hills that spring up from the roads curving along the harbor. The houses, even today, sit close together, and a view into a backyard would reveal vegetable gardens, sheds, bushes, trees, and distant buildings across Smith's Cove to Rocky Neck, much as in Davis's picture.

and-ink drawing *Gloucester Terraces* (plate 28). He exercised great freedom with motifs and repeated them, almost cinematically, to enliven subsequent paintings; for example, women hanging out wash on a line, leaping whippets, and sunflowers appear in *Gloucester Backyard* and several other works. The signage and facade of a favorite automobile garage occur in several paintings, including *Multiple Views* (plate 34). Whatever their degree of abstraction, most of the paintings take off from observed reality but without a fixed viewpoint. Taking his cue from Paul Cézanne's landscapes and the early Cubist works of Pablo Picasso and Georges Braque, Davis jettisoned one-point perspective and piled up the rectangular shapes of tombstones to create *Graveyard—Gloucester* (plate 32). The buildings and streets climbing the Gloucester hills allowed Davis to include a mass of forms in the top register of the canvas rather than a uniformly colored expanse of sky. The results could be a flattened-out crazy quilt, as in *Airview* (plate 33). He could also go all the way to abstraction when he translat-

30. *Gloucester Terraces*

1916. Oil on canvas, 37½ x 29½"
Collection Earl Davis, courtesy
Salander-O'Reilly Galleries, New York

31. *The President*

1917. Oil on canvas, 36 x 26½"
Museum of Art,
Munson-Williams-Proctor
Institute, Utica, New York

ed the rigging of schooners into parallel verticals for his composition *The President* (plate 31).

The artistic practice of experimentation alone made him a "modernist" to F. W. Coburn, the critic from the *Boston Herald,* who wrote about the inaugural exhibition of Gloucester artists held at the Gallery-on-the-Moors in September 1916. To that exhibition Davis submitted *Backyards, Gloucester* and *A Cove,* which Coburn described as a "panoramic perversion" that had "excited much tittering from the uninitiated" at the opening.[36]

Modernism, used as a term of derision by Coburn, was much talked about

44

32. *Graveyard—Gloucester*
1916. Oil on canvas, 23 x 19½"
Collection Earl Davis, courtesy
Salander-O'Reilly Galleries, New York

back in New York during the art seasons of 1916 and 1917. A number of galleries, such as Alfred Stieglitz's at 291 Fifth Avenue, the Modern Gallery, run by Marius de Zayas, the Charles Daniel Gallery, the Bourgeois Galleries, and the Montross Gallery, showed a range of art of interest to those following the new styles. Exhibitions included African art and works by European artists who came to New York to escape World War I.[37]

One exhibition germane to a discussion of Davis was the "Forum Exhibition of Modern American Painters," held during March 1916 at the Anderson Galleries. Willard Huntington Wright, an art critic for *Forum* magazine, organized the exhibition as a showcase for some of the painters working in Cubist and abstract styles. Astute in the art world's politics, he enlisted the help of several of its leaders: Robert Henri, Alfred Stieglitz, John Weischel, who ran the People's Art Guild, magazine editor and painter W. H. de B. Nelson, and the

33. *Airview*

c. 1916. Oil on canvas, 30¼ x 24¼"
Collection Earl Davis, courtesy
Salander-O'Reilly Galleries, New York

34. *Multiple Views*

1918. Oil on canvas, 47 x 35"
Collection Earl Davis, courtesy
Salander-O'Reilly Galleries, New York

Davis painted Multiple Views *at the "Exhibition of Indigenous Painting," held at the Whitney Studio Club in 1918. On September 29, 1953, Davis recalled the circumstances of that novel exhibition to Hermon More, the director of the Whitney Museum of American Art, and John I. H. Baur, then curator of the Whitney. Club members, explained Davis, were invited into the two galleries of the Club headquarters on Fourth Street and confronted with blank canvases of varying sizes that hung on the walls. A table in the center of the room was filled with paints and brushes, whiskey bottles, cigars, and cigarettes. The artists had three days to paint a picture in that atmosphere of drinking and conviviality during which George Luks threatened to overpaint everyone's canvas. Davis described his own picture, which he also called* Gloucester Tour, *as "made out of things I had been painting recently and had in my mind. . . . I had done that kind of composition before that time. . . . composing things that you don't usually see at one time. I have drawings done in that manner."*

critic Christian Brinton, each of whom wrote a foreword. Wright wanted to present an impartial sampling of what he considered "the very best examples of the more modern American art." The goal was "to present for the first time a comprehensive, critical selection of the serious painting now being shown in isolated groups; to turn public attention for the moment from European art and concentrate it on the excellent work being done in America; and to bring serious, deserving painters in direct contact with the public without a commercial intermediary." While Davis was not represented in the show, the ambitious eighty-page catalogue included artists' statements of interest to him, by John Marin, Oscar Bluemner, Arthur G. Dove, Stanton Macdonald-Wright, and Man Ray, among others. All these artists were then struggling to develop a theory

34. *Multiple Views*

based on their own efforts at abstracting images from the real world and setting those into paint. While each statement was unique to that respective artist, the very fact that they were grappling with aesthetic theories might have been an impetus to Davis to articulate his own theories based on his own experiences.[38]

According to John Lane, who has studied in depth the development of Davis's theories, the artist began his theoretical writing on art during these years. Davis inscribed on the reverse of a Gloucester street scene dated 1918: "Cubism is the bridge from percept to concept. A cubist picture is a concept in light and weight of a specific object in nature. It is from that only a step to the expression of a concept of diverse phenomena, sound, touch, light, etc., in a single plastic unit. 14th century demanded plot relationship of subject, 1870 to 1918 demanded plastic relationship of subject. 1918—demands plastic expression of mental scope."[39] This kind of writing reveals that Davis firmly believed in the intellectual nature of art making. Painting might be expression, but it was expression carefully thought through.

At the time no antagonisms concerning matters of art separated the abstractionists from the realists. Groups, circles, and cliques tended to be based on class background and level of sophistication about the European experience, rather than on artistic style. Wealthy collectors such as Louise and Walter Arensberg and Mable Dodge invited European expatriates, such as Marcel Duchamp, and American sophisticates, such as Man Ray, to their dinner parties, whereas Henri, Sloan, and their young realist friends, such as Davis, hung around Romany Marie's, the Greenwich Village Inn, and other cafés open to a working-class clientele. The Henri-Sloan group went to costume balls organized by the *Masses* staff and theater events staged by *Masses* editor Floyd Dell for the Liberal Club.[40] In the mid-teens this group began to join the gatherings at the studio of the wealthy professional sculptor and society matron Gertrude Vanderbilt Whitney. Artists of all artistic persuasions exhibited together at the People's Art Guild, from 1915 to 1918, at the MacDowell Club, and at the March–April 1917 show of the Society of Independent Artists. Davis, whose own style was swinging easily between an expressive Post-Impressionism and semi-abstraction, showed in many of these exhibitions. His first solo exhibition came in December 1917, when the Sheridan Square Gallery mounted his watercolors and drawings, and the following spring he had another exhibition at the Ardsley Gallery in Brooklyn.

As with others of his generation, Davis's most important patron for several decades was Mrs. Whitney, who not only bought the paintings of younger American artists but also contributed generously to organizations promoting contemporary American art. In 1918, with her encouragement, about twenty artists founded the Whitney Studio Club, using two floors of a building she owned on West Fourth Street. The Club became well known for its imaginative group exhibitions, its retrospective exhibitions of artists in need of sales, and its parties, usually presided over by Juliana Force, Mrs. Whitney's associate.[41] Davis always gave the Whitney Studio Club credit for providing "the first place where the American artist was given a real sponsorship, outside of the Academy with its official organs and medals." Mrs. Whitney's belief in "the idea of the free individual artist who had his own right to explore and investigate and find ways outside of the accepted norms of picturemaking" was but a continuation, Davis recalled, of "the whole Henri tradition."[42]

Davis participated in one of the earliest shows held at the Whitney Studio Club in 1918, the "Exhibition of Indigenous Painting," which epitomized the esprit of Club gatherings. Members, including Davis, were invited by Mrs. Force into the two galleries of the Club headquarters on Fourth Street and confronted with blank canvases of varying sizes that hung on the walls. A table in the center of the room was filled with paints and brushes; whiskey bottles, cigars, and cigarettes sustained the artists, who had three days to complete a picture from memory in an atmosphere of drinking and conviviality (a tipsy George Luks threatened to overpaint everyone's canvas). Davis described his own picture, *Multiple Views* (plate 34), then called *Gloucester Tour,* as "made out of things I had been doing recently at Gloucester and had in my mind—several aspects of a landscape all composed in one picture."[43] Davis was referring to the drawing *Gloucester Terraces* (plate 28), a work that would appear new and daring to the modern poet William Carlos Williams in the early 1920s (see below, chapter 2, page 57).

In an age of "little magazines," Davis and his friends caught the bug in late 1916 and founded *Spawn,* a portfolio magazine consisting almost entirely of pictures by contributors who included Glintenkamp, Coleman, Maurice Becker, and John Barber. Some verse appeared on the front cover, while the back cover was printed with a short story by Edmond McKenna. Davis contributed a witty drawing, *Forty Inns on the Lincoln Highway,* little scenes packed together like a cartoon. Although not intended to make money, the magazine got some notice in the newspapers and probably did boost the contributors' reputations among the older vanguard artists and writers in New York's bohemia.[44]

Davis's *Studio Interior* (plate 3) gives us a glimpse into the absorbing life in the studio in the Lincoln Arcade that Davis shared with Glenn Coleman and Henry Glintenkamp. The painting suggests the double influence of Henri Matisse's *Red Studio* of 1911 (The Museum of Modern Art, New York) and Vincent van Gogh's *Bedroom in Arles* of 1888 (Rijksmuseum Vincent van Gogh, Amsterdam), but the subject is clearly Davis's own multipurpose environment. Davis includes among the easel, bed, and furniture the machines of modern life that would absorb his energies almost as much as painting: the typewriter, in the lower right corner, on which he was beginning to write his theories about art; and the Victrola, set against the rear wall, which would provide him with music from his jazz records. The room is a hot orange, while outside the window we glimpse the cool blue world of New York.

Davis's total absorption in the art world was interrupted by army service in 1918. Davis's friend Maurice Becker from *The Masses,* who had been a conscientious objector to the war, went to Mexico to avoid the draft, as did Henry Glintenkamp and poet Robert Carlton Brown. Because of a medical condition, Davis was exempted from active duty, but he was classified for "limited service"

35. *Self-Portrait*

1919. Oil on canvas, 22¼ x 18¼"
Amon Carter Museum, Fort Worth, 1975.29

36. *Yellow Hills*

1919. Oil on canvas, 24 x 30"
The Santa Barbara Museum of Art.
Gift of Heyward Cutting

James Johnson Sweeney, in his catalogue essay for Davis's retrospective exhibition at the Museum of Modern Art in 1945, refers to Yellow Hills *as a Tioga scene. The Tioga landscapes are more brilliant in color, as seems appropriate for summer scenes, than the Gloucester scenes done later that year. But in both, Davis seems to be stepping back from his Cubist experiments of 1915–18, and looking instead to van Gogh.*

and assigned to a branch of Army Intelligence.[45] He had by then returned to live in East Orange, New Jersey, but commuted to Manhattan, where he worked "drafting maps and graphs along ethnographic lines," according to James Johnson Sweeney.[46] These would be used in proposing boundaries for countries and regions once the war was ended.

In the summer of 1919, Davis did not immediately return to Gloucester, perhaps because the Sloans, having decided to travel to the Southwest, were not there. Davis instead went to a farm in Tioga, Pennsylvania, that his mother had rented.[47] Only later, in the fall, did he travel to Gloucester.

In his paintings that summer he appears to have turned his back on the Maratta color system and experimentation with abstract compositions; instead he painted his Tioga landscapes in a style of expressionistic naturalism with bold yellows and bright blues, greens, and reds. Recalling the activated landscapes of van Gogh, Davis's thick, curving strokes of color create the forms of plants, hills, and sun-soaked skies. When he went to Gloucester that fall, he continued to paint landscapes in this style—a retreat from his Cubist interpretations.

And like van Gogh, he also turned to self-portraiture, painting two images of himself with intense scrutiny and bold color contrasts. They were apparently

36. *Yellow Hills*

37. *Dancers on Havana Street*

38. *Night Club, Havana*

1920. Watercolor on paper, 11 x 15"
Rose Art Museum, Brandeis University, Waltham,
Massachusetts. Gift of Teresa Jackson Weill

done on the eve of his departure for Havana with Coleman, when, according to James Johnson Sweeney, he was recuperating from a lingering case of influenza.[48] The sober seriousness with which he takes his own image, so unlike the witty raconteur who told stories at his own expense, suggests that some event, such as a severe illness, did indeed occur.

In December 1919, Davis and Coleman arrived in Havana. The works that Davis did during his Cuban sojourn were watercolors of urban Cubans, in the streets and cafés of Havana. Unlike the earlier, Hoboken series of watercolors, Davis used a range of color within each work and applied color in large flat shapes. Figures are indicated through silhouette rather than by the delineation of their features, and they relate to each other rhythmically—different from the angularity and gridlike format of the Hoboken scenes. The results are decorative splashes of color evocative of the light of a warm climate rather than calculated, narrative genre scenes. After two months, Davis returned with sheaves of sprightly watercolors. He now faced a new decade that would bring more modern European art to New York and that would stimulate more daring experimentation.

37. *Dancers on Havana Street*

1920. Watercolor on paper, 22¾ x 15⅝"
Collection Earl Davis, courtesy
Salander-O'Reilly Galleries, New York

39. *Still Life with "Dial"*

II. Modernist Experimentation: The 1920s

THE 1920S ARE GENERALLY CONSIDERED ONE OF THE conservative eras in American politics, when the country, under the presidencies of Warren Harding and Calvin Coolidge, withdrew into isolationism and retreated from Progressive Era social-reform policies. The decade also witnessed rising prosperity for most Americans, who bought Model-T Fords, radios, and bootleg liquor and put their earnings into the stock market.[1] It was the prosperity, not the conservatism, that created a boom in the arts, and artists devised strategies to promote the new art.

For a short time immediately after the 1918 Armistice, it seemed that the modernist movement might have peaked in New York; many of the European expatriate painters had returned to France and some galleries had closed. However, by 1920 it became clear that experimental styles in painting and sculpture were here to stay. Older, established galleries began to show the new work; for example, Knoedler exhibited Morton Schamberg's machine abstractions in 1919. And new, proselytizing organizations took up the cause. Most notable and long-lasting was the Société Anonyme, the brainchild of Marcel Duchamp, Joseph Stella, Man Ray, and the painter and art patron Katherine S. Dreier. The organizers opened a gallery on East Forty-seventh Street in 1920 and during the next few years showed the work of primarily European artists—Constructivists, Suprematists, and Dadaists, including Kurt Schwitters, Piet Mondrian, Max Ernst, Kazimir Malevich, Vasily Kandinsky, Fernand Léger, and Alexander Archipenko—and eventually a number of Americans.[2] Another organization, which set itself up as the American counterpart to the Société Anonyme, was Modern Artists of America, a group of thirty-nine American artists who exhibited together at the Joseph Brummer Galleries in 1922. Davis joined the group along with Joseph Stella, the poet and artist E. E. Cummings, the critic and artist Hamilton Easter Field, and many Whitney Studio Club artists. The catalogue of their 1922 show declared:

The time [has] come to gather together the various elements opposed to academic art, and the Modern Artists of America is the first society which has brought together the forces opposed to the blind acceptance of tradition. . . . The conservative artists have in the Academy a bulwark against all experimental art, against all change. The radical artists now have a society which, giving experimental art a place, cannot fail to influence profoundly the future of art. The spirit of life, of fearlessness, of joy, of restlessness which animates so much of the work of the younger men will be able to make itself felt.[3]

39. *Still Life with "Dial"*

1922. Oil on canvas, 50 x 32"
Collection Earl Davis, courtesy
Salander-O'Reilly Galleries, New York

In December 1926, Davis had a retrospective exhibition of forty-three paintings at the Whitney Studio Club. Four still-life paintings were shown, all dated 1922, which might have included Still Life with "Dial" *and* Three Table Still Life *(plate 48).*

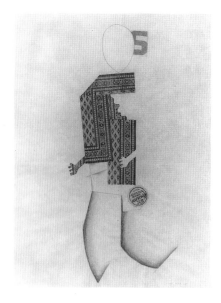

40. *Untitled*

1921. Pencil and collage on paper,
22½ x 16½"
Collection Earl Davis, courtesy
Salander-O'Reilly Galleries, New York

41. *ITLKSEZ*

1921. Watercolor and collage on paper, 22 x 16"
Museum of Fine Arts, Boston.
The William H. Lane Collection

While Davis absorbed the lessons of Cubism, he could also poke fun at its pretensions. With the title, short for "It looks easy," he shows the economy of modernism with both a sentence and an image abbreviated from conventional representation.

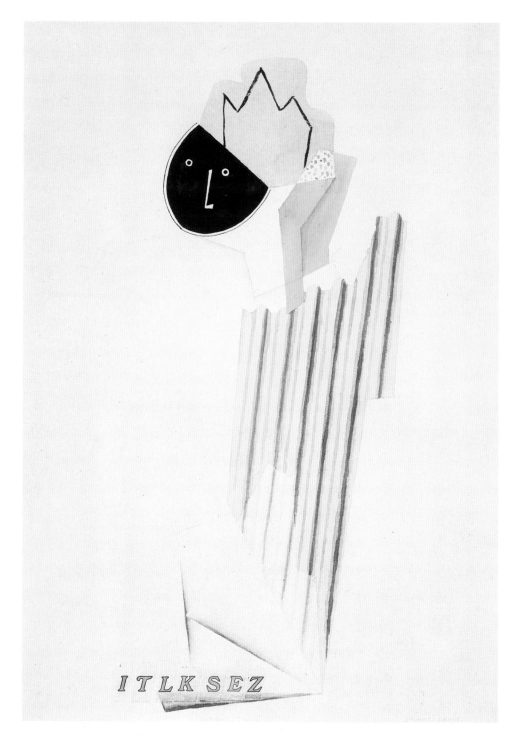

The statement reiterates many of the themes of the artists who had participated in the Armory Show and the Independents show of 1910 and who had been associated with *The Masses*. A general spirit of "experimentation," rather than any one specific "ism," best characterized the program of these modern artists.

Thus, early in 1920, when Davis returned from a two-month stay in Cuba, he was at the beginning of a decade when his own experiments would find a sympathetic audience. Not only could Davis see more new art, in 1920 he came into greater contact with the literary modernists, and this, too, propelled him away from the Post-Impressionist landscapes of Tioga and toward acts of greater pictorial daring.

In 1920, two avant-garde journals published his drawings. *The Dial,* a literary magazine revamped in 1920 into a leading journal for modernist writers, published four of Davis's drawings in its August 1920 issue. These imaginary portraits of Fyodor Dostoyevsky, Theodore Dreiser, John Synge, and Alexander Ostrovsky recalled his "Ashcan" drawings done for *The Masses* in the mid-teens, and as such were far more traditional than the art of Charles Demuth, John Marin, and Jules Pascin, also published in *The Dial.* At the same time, *The Little Review,* which had been serializing excerpts from James Joyce's *Ulysses,* published a whimsical line drawing by Davis for its July–August issue. Davis's contribution, "Composers of Musical Comedies," looks like an Art Young cartoon for *The Masses;* it has none of the avant-garde qualities upon which the journal prided itself. But contacts with these journals brought his art to the attention of the leading new poets. That summer he met the poet William Carlos Williams, an event which no doubt strengthened his resolve to side with the experimental modernists and to begin thinking of painting as primarily the expressive construction of color and space relations.

Williams, a pediatrician from Paterson, New Jersey, and a friend of Demuth's, belonged to the New York literary avant-garde. Casting about for a suitable illustration for a book of poetry, *Kora in Hell: Improvisations,* he took a fancy to one of Davis's drawings. Williams recalled: "I had seen a drawing by Stuart Davis, a young artist I had never met, which I wanted reproduced in my book because it was as close as possible to my idea of the Improvisations. It was, graphically, exactly what I was trying to do in words, put the Improvisations down as a unit on the page. . . . Floss [Williams's wife] and I went to Gloucester and got permission from Stuart Davis to use his art—an impressionistic view of the simultaneous."[4] Williams rewarded Davis with a copy of the book upon its publication. The artist responded on September 18, 1920, with a note of thanks and praised Williams's originality: "I see in it a fluidity as opposed to stagnation of presentation. . . . It opens a field of possibilities. To me it suggests a development toward word against word without any impediments of story, poetic beauty or anything at all except word clash and sequence. This may be a total misrepresentation of your motives. Best of all the work does not suggest any of the modern poets with whom I am familiar. I like the book and am glad to be associated with it."[5] "Fluidity," "word clash," and "sequence" were concepts that Davis would pursue throughout the rest of his career. But since he was a visual artist, to the category of "word clash" we must add "visual motifs"—signs which act to sight as words do to hearing.

His comments to Williams bring to the surface the thoughts he had about his own painting. The fact that "the simultaneous" occupied him is evidenced by a notation, dated May 1920, in a journal he kept in the years 1920–22. With this entry he makes the point that "In looking at nature we do not analyze the drawing and color separately. It is one thing and a simultaneous impression."[6]

It is not known for certain when he began keeping the journals in which

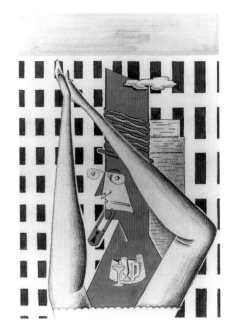

42. *Untitled*

1923. Mixed media and watercolor on paper, 14½ x 9½"
Collection Earl Davis, courtesy
Salander-O'Reilly Galleries, New York

43. *Cocktail Time*

1925 (dated 1926). Gouache on paper, 12 x 8½". Private collection

44. *Lucky Strike*

1921. Oil on canvas, 33¼ x 18″
The Museum of Modern Art, New York. Gift of
The American Tobacco Company, Inc., 1951

*During the 1960s this painting was
often reproduced as a prototype to Pop
Art, since the subject refers to a popular
artifact of everyday life—tobacco. To an
alert audience in the 1920s, the painting blended the elegance of European
collage Cubism, and its composition of
overlaying flat planes, with the assert-
iveness of American advertising and
commercial packaging. However, the
painting, like others in Davis's Tobacco
series, did not advance his theories of
space-color.*

45. *Sweet Caporal*

1922. Watercolor and oil on canvas, 20 x 18½"
Thyssen-Bornemisza Collection, Madrid

46. *Landscape*

1922. Oil on board, 15¾ x 11½″
Collection Earl Davis, courtesy
Salander-O'Reilly Galleries, New York

This work has been alternately titled
Motif *for* "Combination Concrete,"
because Davis appropriated the shapes
for his later 1958 painting. Many com-
positions of the 1920s were recycled for
the imagery of Davis's 1950s paintings.

he systematically wrote down the theories he was formulating regarding artistic practice. The surviving typed and handwritten records, loose and bound, exceed ten thousand pages.[7] Sometimes his writings function as "how-to" guidelines for the laying out of a composition or the application of paint. Often he devotes long passages to the basic elements of a painting (line, shape, color), composition (the two-dimensional design), and space (the representation of three-dimensional illusionism). Sometimes the entries make broad generalizations about the relationship of art to society, particularly those passages from the 1930s, when he attempted to reconcile Marxist theory with his own experiences of artistic practice. He often makes lists of the everyday objects that inter-

MODERNIST EXPERIMENTATION

47. *The Coast*

1921. Oil on canvas, 20 x 40"
Collection Earl Davis, courtesy
Salander-O'Reilly Galleries, New York

ested him in his environment, yet he is never a cultural nationalist seeking the "essence" of "American character" or trumpeting the superiority of his own country. Through all these journal pages, we can see him attempting to justify his own kind of painting—as both artistic, with a capital A, and as something that in principle ought to be understood by everyone. And while at times he can be serious and badgering, at other times he is playful and self-deprecating.

The 1920–22 notebook sets down many of the themes that he would take up in the later notebooks. And behind the arguments and dictums hover the figures of Robert Henri and John Sloan, artists who believed that, above all, art should communicate the experience of contemporary life. Davis wrote in his May 1920 entry: "A realistic picture gives an opportunity for the complete expression of one phase of an object whereas an aggregation of symbols may express many phases, incongruity, or in other words[,] a greater sense of life." He was acutely aware of his time and place, a twentieth-century America offering stimulating new experiences to the artist. Hence, the artist could no longer rely on the discoveries of the past to meet present needs: "Light and shade in the impressionistic sense must be dropped and in their place plastic proportions must be used with the aid of textures."[8]

And yet for all the rules he was formulating, he cautioned himself: "As regards theories and formulas like the above and their use in actual work the following thought occurs. If your picture is merely a chart illustrating these premises it will be lifeless. The theory must be burned in the fires of reality before it becomes alive—so—in painting if you want to do something other than the rules you have laid down[,] do not hesitate for an instant—but—the thinking in terms of these rules will give a speed & momentum to your work you

48. *Three Table Still Life*

1922. Oil on canvas, 42 x 32"
Collection Edward J. Lenkin

could not otherwise have."[9] Such cautions about rules might have arisen, in part, from his reaction to the unquestioned enthusiasm of his colleagues for Hardesty Maratta's color system or Jay Hambidge's theories of "dynamic symmetry."

This 1920–22 notebook also makes clear that he thinks paintings must be different from "illustrations": "The separation of the idea of representing a psychological or literary conception (illustration) from the representation of lighted forms in space must be insisted on. An illustration represents an aspect of character. A painting deals only with the 3 dimensional realities regardless of local character."[10] Davis's pronouncement about illustration would serve to

MODERNIST EXPERIMENTATION

explain why the naturalistic drawings—like the "Ashcan" graphics he was then submitting to *The Dial*—coexist in time with his experiments in painting with light, form, color, and a freer use of abstraction. The double standard of guidelines different for illustration from those for painting recalls Sloan's own vow to keep his "message" art—his political drawings and cartoons—in a separate category from his painting. To Davis, like Sloan before him, painting meant the serious working out of pictorial problems. This did not mean that Davis thought any less of illustration; on the contrary, in a notebook entry of 1922 he reminded himself: "A living can be made out of illustrations. Do them!"[11]

If his art practice lagged behind his theories, he was nonetheless making art at a frantic pace. In April 1921 he exhibited at the Whitney Studio Club along with Joaquín Torres-García and Stanislaw Szukalski. Henry McBride, who reviewed the show for the *New York Sunday Herald*, called Davis "one of the most considerable 'modernists' in the city": "His work is excellent in every way, in color, in design and, better than all, in exuberant and irresistible enthusiasm."[12] While Davis was not the only young American artist attempting to work out new styles for a new technological age, he could easily have been the most vocal and single-minded—at least in the eyes of Rudi Blesh, who wrote in 1960: "Stuart Davis took up abstraction in 1921; one by one, others joined him: Arthur B. Carles, Jan Matulka, John Graham, Vaclav Vytlacil, Arshile Gorky."[13] None of the other five artists mentioned by Blesh exhibited with the Modern Artists of America in their show of 1922. Obviously, groups of artists working in the modern style were springing up all over town, and Davis would soon get to know them.

During the rest of 1921 and extending into 1922, Davis took his modernist experiments in three distinct directions: small, often witty, mixed media collages on paper; a series of very original oil paintings adopting the imagery and graphics of tobacco packaging; and Cubist landscape and still-life paintings along the lines of the work of Pablo Picasso, Georges Braque, Juan Gris, and Diego Rivera.

The mixed-media collages that Davis began in 1921 combined pasted papers, pencil, ink, charcoal, watercolor, and gouache. Collage techniques were well known in New York, with examples frequently on display in the galleries by such artists as Picasso, Kurt Schwitters, Arthur Dove, and Joseph Stella. It looked easy to Davis, so he tried his hand at it. One result was his witty collage entitled *ITLKSEZ*, abbreviated from "It looks easy" (see plate 41). Into the mid-1920s, Davis could not resist using collage techniques to make sprightly drawings of top-hatted figures, out on the town, chasing women. Works such as an untitled collage (plate 40) and *Cocktail Time* (plate 43) recall the ultrasophisticated, but still tongue-in-cheek humor of *Smart Set* magazine and Cole Porter tunes.[14]

The series of Cubist compositions that appropriated the imagery of the packaging of tobacco products included *Lucky Strike* of 1921 (plate 44) and *Sweet Caporal* of 1922 (plate 45). These oil paintings are not collages (i.e., papers pasted down on a support), but are meant to look like collages, much in the spir-

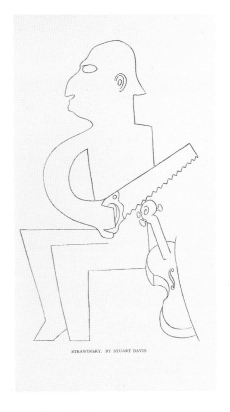

STRAWINSKY. BY STUART DAVIS

49. *Strawinsky*

Published in *The Dial* 73 (August 1922), opp. p. 158

50. *Mexican Girls*

1923. Oil on artist's board
(or canvas), 20 x 16⅛″
Collection Earl Davis, courtesy
Salander-O'Reilly Galleries, New York

For a handful of figural compositions done in New Mexico, Davis experimented with several tones of one or two hues, in this case warm gray. Contrary to his usual practice of using color to suggest space, here the tones seem decorative, to balance the four quadrants of the painting.

it of the Synthetic Cubist works by Picasso and Braque. At the same time, the collages of Kurt Schwitters were shown at the galleries of the Société Anonyme in 1920 and 1921. Hence, collages and pseudo-collages were continually on view. But, as pointed out by the art historian Barbara Zabel, the differences between all these artists are telling. The French artists used imagery to create a café and studio atmosphere, while Schwitters presented the materials "as nothing more than the detritus of a modern consumer society with throw-away habits."[15] Davis, unlike Picasso, Braque, or Schwitters, used the imagery to suggest the worlds of advertising and product promotion, and he did so in an upbeat way at the very time when the United States was becoming the world leader in advertising. Davis knew what he was doing; in his words, he wanted to be "rigorously logical. American not French." He considered his Tobacco series to be "an original note without parallel" and "really original American work."[16]

To an artist like Davis, making a living through advertising and commercial work hardly differed from selling illustrations and cartoons to the journals. At a time when the advertising industry was hiring many New York artists, such as Edward Hopper, Rockwell Kent, and the photographer Edward Steichen, it was also raising standards of artistic quality. One effective way to do this was through citations and awards. None other than Davis's mentor, Robert Henri, was invited to judge the first advertising art exhibition sponsored by the Art Directors Club of New York in 1921.[17] Davis saw that an artist could learn valuable lessons from the innovations in graphic design at the service of advertising. In spite of his pronouncement that illustration and painting should follow different standards of art making, Davis thought a great deal about the overlapping of popular or commercial art with the fine arts. On June 1, 1921, he wrote, "The best adds [*sic*] to-day have as their dominant assets—high visibility and that is a quality for which I have long striven."[18]

As a firmly modern man, one who believed that art should communicate the everyday experiences of the new technological age, Davis could never be accused of promulgating an art for the élite. He wanted his art to be popular both in its clearly recognizable subject matter and in its immediate appeal to a broad audience, much as advertising sought to do. He might have even toyed with the idea of earning a living as a commercial artist, an occupation he would not have disparaged, but simply would have preferred not to pursue. In one of the many instances in which he admits the practical necessity of earning a living, he admonishes himself: "The new point of view says, 'What will sell?' Get a point of view that the people can understand and then do it better than anybody else. . . . You want to get ahead. Very well then accept don't fight—let your art be the satisfaction & paint subjects that people want. . . . Never mind El Greco, Picasso or any of the others . . . attend to the needs of Stuart Davis which are now primarily financial."[19]

While Davis's Tobacco series referred to the imagery of mass-produced packaging, he chose to paint brands of cigarette papers and loose tobacco—coded as part of a distinctly masculine world. Even though some women smoked, their cigarettes were always pre-rolled; only men rolled their own. Barbara Zabel, whose study of Davis's Tobacco pictures includes a thorough analysis of changes in the marketing of tobacco, points out that the cigarette (handrolled or not), even while under attack by the prohibitionists, had become a patriotic symbol. American troops fighting overseas had been sent large quantities of Bull Durham tobacco by the American Tobacco Company. Smoking also became part of Davis's personal persona; all who knew him recall a perpetual cigarette dangling from his mouth.[20]

The Tobacco paintings consist of flat, overlapping shapes that suppress the illusion of three-dimensional space; the unity of these paintings comes from this flatness as well as from bold color and lively design. However, Davis's theoretical interests were at the time pointing in another direction; he wanted to create a

51. Fernand Léger. *Three Women*

1921. Oil on canvas, 6′ ¼″ x 8′ 3″
The Museum of Modern Art, New York.
Mrs. Simon Guggenheim Fund

Léger's painting was reproduced in The Little Review *in the spring of 1923, to accompany his article entitled "The Aesthetics of the Machine: Manufactured Objects, Artisan and Artist." Davis, then experimenting with his own art, would have taken a great interest in Léger's ideas and imagery.*

52. *New Mexican Landscape*

1923. Oil on canvas, 32 x 40¼"
Amon Carter Museum, Fort Worth

53. Stuart Davis
in New Mexico, 1923

new pictorial space, the classic problem for modern painters.[21] In page after page of his early notebooks, we see him struggling toward a coherent theory of art that would integrate his belief in painting as an art of color with his modern grasp of spatial relations. At one point, perhaps in 1923, he wrote: "My original interest in character has waned, drawing the subject in front of me with more or less 'feeling' is a thing that no longer creates in me a desire to work. I am interested in a new sense of space and have not yet succeeded in getting it sufficiently clear in my mind to feel at home with it."[22] Though formally beautiful, the Tobacco paintings became a dead end for Davis, since they did not advance his thinking about spatial relations.

He was more successful in this regard with his landscapes and still lifes of the early 1920s, where the objects that generated his pictorial imagery—rocks, gas pumps, and schooners—are themselves three dimensional. In a painting such as *The Coast* of 1921 (plate 47), he introduced dashed strokes of color in the area of the sea. While they can be regarded as conventionally representing waves or ripples on the sea surface, the uniformity of stroke tends to flatten the composition; the textured surface resulting from the dashes creates another kind of color that plays off against flat areas. In the more modest *Landscape* of 1922 (plate 46), the areas of painted dashes, speckles, and spots fit together like the discrete sections of a jigsaw puzzle. The clues to its "landscape" nature come less from the spatial recession (almost nonexistent) or from the imagery, such as the outlines and silhouettes of trees, than from the road signs that tell us to GO SLOW or to expect a CURVE. Later in his career, in the 1940s and 1950s, he would return to the compositional structure of these early works when developing other paintings.[23]

Also in 1922, Davis painted monumental still-life compositions that are the most European he had done so far. Davis used color, tonal values, texture, and space decoratively when he painted *Three Table Still Life* (plate 48) and *Still Life*

54. *Egg Beater*

1923. Oil on canvas, 37 x 22"
Collection Earl Davis, courtesy
Salander-O'Reilly Galleries, New York

with *"Dial"* (plate 39), much as Picasso, Gris, and Rivera had done in their equally colorful, large Synthetic Cubist oils. The stippled areas of *Three Table Still Life* recall Picasso's still lifes of 1913–14. The large repeating forms remind us of Gris's and Rivera's elegant paintings of the late teens and early twenties.

Clearly Davis needed a break from the intensity of these experiments. Thus, in the summer of 1923, when Dolly and John Sloan invited him and his brother, Wyatt, to accompany them on a drive to Santa Fe, New Mexico, he must have accepted eagerly. The four went off, in the Sloan's Model-T Ford (see plate 53), to the desert town that had long been a retreat for New York artists, who were attracted both to the scenery—mesas, spectacular skies, and unbroken horizons—and to the unfamiliar culture of the Pueblo tribes. Robert Henri had first visited Santa Fe in 1916; Leon Kroll, one of Sloan's students in Gloucester, had gone there in 1917. The Sloans went to Santa Fe in 1919 and not only immersed themselves in the art colony but also became enthusiasts of American Indian arts and crafts. Sloan in fact sent a group of watercolors by American Indian artists to the Society of Independent Artists exhibition in New York in 1920.[24] Nearby Taos also attracted artists and writers, such as D. H. Lawrence and Mable Dodge. East Coast artists who made the trek to either Santa Fe or Taos included Andrew Dasburg, Marsden Hartley, Victor Higgins, John Marin, Jan Matulka, and Georgia O'Keeffe.

Davis found the scenery beautiful and the indigenous material fascinating, but he could not paint it. Recounting his New Mexico experience to James Johnson Sweeney, he wrote of the three or so months he spent there: "I . . . did not do much work because the place itself was so interesting. I don't think you could do much work there except in a literal way, because the place is always there in such a dominating way. You always have to look at it. Then there's the great dead population. You don't see them but you stumble over them. A piece of pottery here and there and everywhere. It's a place for an ethnologist not an artist. Not sufficient intellectual stimulus. Forms made to order, to imitate. Colors—but I never went there again."[25] Davis was not alone in his reaction to the Southwest. Edward Hopper also visited Santa Fe, in 1925, at Sloan's urging. Like Davis, Hopper did not find the place conducive to his art, and he never returned. What the Santa Fe scenery lacked for Davis's visual imagination were the vertical coordinates provided by the schooners, tall spires, and trees of Gloucester or the soaring skyscrapers of Manhattan. In his few landscapes of New Mexico, he controlled the limitless space by enclosing the scenes with the storybook frames one sees in children's book illustrations (see plate 52).

Even in New Mexico, Davis continued to explore his ideas about space-color compositions. He developed a series of small oil-on-board figural paintings, composed of flat areas of gray with some color, such as *Indian Family* of 1923 (collection Earl Davis) and *Interior* of 1923 (collection Earl Davis). With *Mexican Girls* (plate 50), Davis used only a warm pewter gray hue in four tonal variations, but suggested yet other tones through stippling darker gray over lighter gray. The human subjects, like the landscapes, have a decorative, storybook quality.

Davis was more successful in a series of still-life compositions begun in New Mexico of single objects, such as a saw or an egg beater (see plate 54). In these almost monochromatically blue paintings, he again created the illusion of additional tones by developing areas with short dashes of paint. While the landscapes and the figural compositions were stylistic dead ends, the subjects of the still lifes generated other ideas and paintings. In New York during 1924 and

55. *Odol*

1924. Oil on cardboard, 24 x 18"
Cincinnati Art Museum.
The Edwin and Virginia Irwin Memorial

1925, Davis continued to make still-life compositions that contained a limited number of objects: a lemon, a drinking glass or two, a jug, a bottle of Odol, an electric bulb. The resulting paintings contain elegant shapes true to their real forms; the heavy black outlining recalls some of the contemporaneous compositions of Fernand Léger. Davis uses reductive modeling to give three-dimensional depth to the transparent glasses and light bulbs, and provides the equivalent of color variety by overlaying adjacent planes with painted grids, stripes, dashes, and stippled dots (see plates 55 and 57).

Following his usual routine, Davis returned to Gloucester in the summers

56. *Super Table*

1925. Oil on canvas, 48½ x 34⅛"
Terra Museum of American Art, Chicago.
Daniel J. Terra Collection, 8.1986

and early fall months throughout the early and mid-1920s to paint the harbors, docks, and boats. He even went there following his New Mexico trip. According to the artist Theresa Bernstein, in 1923 Davis and his family lived in the same East Gloucester summer cottage with Bernstein and her husband, William Meyerowitz. Shortly after Bernstein and Meyerowitz bought their place on Mount Pleasant Avenue (up the hill from the Red Cottage), the Davises also bought a place on the same road. Bernstein recalled that Romany Marie, a friend of the Henri crowd, ran the Village Tea Room in East Gloucester, which offered the burgeoning artists' colony a bohemian place to congregate.[26]

57. *Edison Mazda*

1924. Oil on cardboard, 24½ x 18⅝"
The Metropolitan Museum of Art, New York.
Purchase, Mr. and Mrs. Clarence Y. Palitz, Jr.,
Gift, in memory of her father, Nathan Dobson,
1982 (1982.10)

Davis was a fixture of the Gloucester summer art scene and could be seen roaming the hills and exploring the docks with sketchbook in hand. In 1922, he had even jumped into local art politics. When conservative artists organized a North Shore Arts Association, Davis, Alice and Charles Winter, and others organized a more democratically run alternative group, the Gloucester Society of Arts. As the chairman of the new group, Davis was singled out by the local *Gloucester Daily Times:* "Stuart Davis of New York . . . is of the democratic type, with the sympathy of non-limitations to the painter."[27] The Davis group favored juryless exhibitions. However, when the Gloucester Society of Arts held its first exhibition, consisting of 125 paintings, in July 1923, Davis's work was absent—

　MODERNIST EXPERIMENTATION

not surprisingly, since his New Mexico trip had interrupted his Gloucester ties.

By the mid-1920s, Davis had accumulated a substantial body of work, enough for a good-size exhibition. In February 1925, he had his first solo museum exhibition, at the Newark Museum. In October 1926, he participated in a group show at the Charles Daniel Gallery. From an exhibition that included George Ault, Glenn Coleman, Stefan Hirsch, and Reginald Marsh, the critic for the *New York Evening Sun* singled Davis out as "the only avowed cubist among [them]. . . . He has all the decorative certainty of other painters in the abstract and adds something they have not—a touch of humor."[28]

Davis's big break, however, came in December 1926, when he had a two-week retrospective exhibition at the Whitney Studio Club. As he later recalled, the plan for the retrospective had a casual beginning—probably the suggestion of his friend Joseph Pollet to Juliana Force. Pollet had been storing Davis's paintings in his studio, a space on the top floor of the Club's location at 14 West Eighth Street. The rationale for the show was to help Davis sell at a time when he "was dead broke and had no place to work" other than the small, eight-by-eleven-foot room in which he lived.[29] Spread out in two large galleries were forty-three paintings, including several of the Hoboken watercolors, New England landscapes, a Tioga landscape, two Cuban watercolors, four large still-life paintings of 1922, several works done in New Mexico, and still-life paintings of the mid-1920s. Since the point of the exhibition was sales—indeed five paintings were sold from the show—Force resisted including Davis's most recent experimental work.

Nevertheless, the critics sensed Davis's range. The *New York Evening Post* commented: "His work covers a number of varying experimental periods and registers sincere best in the experiments. That nothing very decisive comes out of it all probably is quite negligible to Mr. Davis since he is still in the throes of theory and undecided himself as to his aesthetic credo of procedure." In another review, a critic observed:

Often his work appears to be what John Sloan might call laboratory work. An aesthetic idea from within himself concerns him less than the demonstration of an idea already expressed.

This is what must happen in our day of over theorizing. The theory becomes the thing. . . . He is a son of the age of painting experimentation. He has experimented for years. If that is his bent why not?

This exhibition has an air of saying: Here are the results of years of experimentation. It leaves unanswered the question as to what the artist will produce as the fruit of his examination of many different changing and opposing tendencies.[30]

The reviews must have helped to persuade Juliana Force that Davis needed time to consolidate some of his ideas and practices. Both Mrs. Whitney and Force knew that experimentation, necessary though it is, usually works against sales, since cautious patrons prefer artists who have developed a signature style. It is to the credit of both women that in early 1927, right after Davis's exhibition

58. *Table with Easel*

1925. Ink on paper, 13 x 9½"
Collection Earl Davis, courtesy
Salander-O'Reilly Galleries, New York

59. *Myopic Vista*

1925. Watercolor on paper, 15⅜ x 18″ (sight)
Museum of Fine Arts, Boston.
Gift of the William Lane Foundation

at the Whitney Studio Club, Mrs. Whitney began to send him an allowance of 125 dollars a month—an arrangement that lasted a year.[31] This relieved him of the financial anxieties always present for artists lacking trust funds or working spouses, and allowed him to concentrate his energies on developing his own theoretical understanding of space and color and pushing his experiments to some sort of conclusion.

In the works of 1927 and 1928, Davis turned from natural forms and landscapes to sharp-edged abstractions with clear colors and machinelike forms. The stimulus for this development might have come from many quarters. The large international exhibition of modern paintings sponsored by the Société Anonyme held at the Brooklyn Museum, and then at the Anderson Galleries in Manhattan, in the winter of 1926–27 created a stir. Marcel Duchamp chose works for the show with advisors who included Kandinsky, Mondrian, Schwitters, and Léger. Another influence might have been the "Machine-Age Exposition," organized by Jane Heap of *The Little Review* and held in New York in May 1927, which displayed works by Russian, Belgian, French, Austrian, German, Polish, and American architects, sculptors, painters, and industrial designers.[32] Louis Lozowick's bold black-and-white abstract designs, called *Machine Ornaments,* reproduced in the catalogue and shown at the Exposition, were not unlike Davis's contemporaneous drawings in pen and ink. Man Ray's *Revolving Doors,* first done as collages in 1916–17 and published as prints in 1926 (see plate 61),

60. *Early American Landscape*

1925. Oil on canvas, 19 x 22"
Whitney Museum of American Art,
New York. Gift of Juliana Force

IV

61. Man Ray, *The Meeting* from
the portfolio *Revolving Doors*

1926. Color pochoir, 22 x 15"
Whitney Museum of American Art,
New York. Purchase, 72.84

are close prototypes for the oil paintings Davis would produce in 1927, such as
Percolator (plate 62) and *Matches* (The Chrysler Museum, Norfolk, Virginia). It
is inconceivable that Davis would not have seen such well-publicized shows
and studied the latest in European art; he himself was included in a Société
Anonyme exhibition in 1928, and at least one reviewer felt he "holds his own"

62. *Percolator*

1927. Oil on canvas, 36 x 29"
The Metropolitan Museum of Art, New York.
Arthur Hoppock Hearn Fund, 1956 (56.195)

Edith Halpert gave enormous encouragement to the artists who showed in her gallery, and Davis carried on a correspondence with her during the years he was associated with her. On August 11, 1927, he wrote about his art and the underlying three-dimensional illusionism of all painting, whether called realist or abstract: "In the first place my purpose is to make Realistic pictures. I insist upon this definition in spite of the fact that the type of work I am now doing is generally spoken of as Abstraction. The distinction is important in that it may lead people to realize that they are to look at what is there instead of hunting for symbolic suggestions. A picture is always a three-dimensional illusion regardless of subject matter. That is to say that the most illustrative types of painting and modern so-called abstractions are identical in that they both represent an illusion of the three-dimensional space of our experience. They differ in subject which means that they choose a different character of space to represent. People must be made to realize that in looking at Abstractions they are looking at pictures as objective and as realistic in intent as those commonly accepted as such. I think this point is important and not generally understood."

among the company of Kandinsky, Léger, Paul Klee, and Giorgio de Chirico.[33] Moreover, *The Little Review* and other art magazines were filled with reproductions of machine imagery.

Davis had an opportunity to test some of his pictures on a critical audience when the dealer Edith Halpert, owner of the Downtown Gallery, gave him an exhibition in late November and early December 1927 that showcased his new work. The critic for the *New York Times* attempted to explain Davis's use of the word "real" to describe such works as *Percolator* and *Matches*:

To [Davis] "Percolator" is not seen from a photographic viewpoint, but as the interrelation of variously intersecting planes, the result to be judged solely by the effectiveness of the harmony and the design.

65. *Egg Beater No. 3*

1928. Oil on canvas, 25 x 39″
Museum of Fine Arts, Boston. Gift of the
William H. Lane Foundation, 1990.391

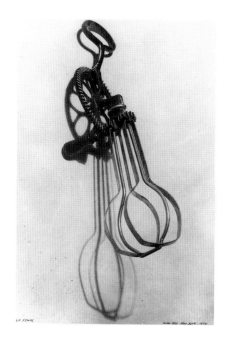

63. Man Ray. *Woman*

1918. Photograph.
Musée National d'Art Moderne,
Centre Georges Pompidou, Paris

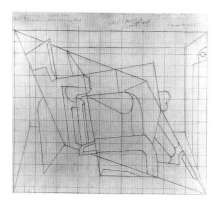

64. Drawing for *Egg Beater No. 2*

1928. Pencil on paper, 15 x 20″
Collection Earl Davis, courtesy
Salander-O'Reilly Galleries, New York

On this ground Mr. Davis's achievements must be qualified. While his decorative intent is realized in the simplified compositions, "Three Objects" and the two still life drawings, it loses clarity in the more complicated design, until in "Matches" and "Percolator" it seems quite incomprehensible.[34]

The critic was at least beginning to see Davis's art in the artist's own terms.

The constant carping from critics about his freewheeling, far-ranging experimentation must have had an impact on Davis's decision to pursue the direction begun in *Percolator* and *Matches*. Since he needed to settle down and concentrate, he created a project for himself—the Egg Beater series—on which he worked during 1927 and early 1928. As he explained to Sweeney in 1945, the Egg Beater paintings commenced when he "nailed an electric fan, a rubber glove and an eggbeater to a table." For a year he limited himself to the exercise of developing compositions based on a series of planes suggested by those particular geometrical shapes. He did not aim to eliminate reality, but "to strip a subject down to the real physical source of its stimulus." To Davis, the series was not to be regarded "as the future aspect of all my painting, but rather as a groping towards a structural concept."[35] By thus concentrating his experiments on the geometric elements of the objects and on the recession of the planes that defined them, Davis created four elegant paintings, along with several studies and drawings. The palette of these Egg Beater paintings blends pastels and fully saturated hues—which became progressively bolder as he approached the fourth and last in the series. Shapes are connected by apparent lines, which, on close examination, as for example in *Egg Beater No. 3* (plate 65), turn out to be the spaces between the shapes, or, to put it another way, the ground on which the flat shapes rest.

All four Egg Beater paintings made their debut at the Valentine Gallery in April and May 1928, in a two-artist exhibition Davis shared with Glenn Cole-

66. *Egg Beater No. 1*

1927. Oil on canvas, 29⅛ x 36″
Whitney Museum of American Art, New York.
Gift of Gertrude Vanderbilt Whitney, 31.169

67. *Egg Beater No. 2*

1928. Oil on canvas, 29¼ x 36¼″
Collection Mr. and Mrs. James A. Fisher,
Pittsburgh

68. Photograph of Place Pasdeloup, Paris

69. *Place Pasdeloup*

1928. Oil on canvas, 36¼ x 28¾"
Whitney Museum of American Art, New York.
Gift of Gertrude Vanderbilt Whitney, 31.170

Place Pasdeloup *is characteristic of Davis's Paris scenes, with its composition of layered building facades, simplified fenestration, prominent signage, Dufy-esque squiggles, and palette of pastel colors.*

man. The critic for the *New York Sun* compared Davis favorably to European artists: "Lately, Mr. Davis suppressed all frivolity, and concerns himself strictly with ideas of beauty. He has a relationship to the teachings of Juan Gris, Picasso and Braque, but manages to conserve a flavor of his own. He is not as plastic in his painting as Gris but he has a cool elegance and assurance that is attractive. He has probably arrived at being the best among the Americans who paint on themes from the abstract, which is fortunate for him, since there seems to be a renewed interest here in such work."[36] Davis was clearly rising in the estimation of the critics.

After the Valentine Gallery show, Force bought *New Mexican Landscape* and *Early American Landscape* for Mrs. Whitney and urged Davis to go abroad. With 900 dollars from Mrs. Whitney, Davis set out. He recalled:

I guess she [Mrs. Whitney] was sorry for me because I was about the only one in the [Whitney Studio] Club who hadn't been to France and she thought it would be good for me. I didn't ask her for the money but I accepted it gratefully and was on the next boat over. What with a little more money she gave me later, I was able to stay in Paris for over a year and I really worked hard instead of sitting in the cafés all day the way some Americans did. I did my share of that too, but I still managed to produce about a dozen paintings which were decent enough to be looked at, as well as some lithographs. It was a very profitable experience and I gave Mrs. Force three of my best pictures when I came back.[37]

The Paris sojourn was just what he needed. It put him in touch with a set of sophisticated American expatriate artists, introduced him to leading avant-garde French artists whom he had long admired, and made him realize "the enormous vitality of the American atmosphere as compared to Europe."[38]

Davis arrived in France in mid-June 1928, bringing with him two of the Egg Beater paintings. In his 1945 autobiography he related an amusing anecdote about being detained at the border by a French customs agent who was somewhat suspicious about the importation of the paintings. Davis explained to the agent that he had done them "in the style of Cubism" and that "it was necessary for my artistic serenity to have them about at all times as a source of inspiration. . . . I had struck the right note,—'ah, Cubism,' he said, 'but of course,' and signed an immediate release. This pleasantly terse exchange confirmed my view that I had come to the right place."[39]

Davis moved into the studio that Jan Matulka was just vacating at 50 Rue Vercingétorix in the Montparnasse district, an area where dozens of artists lived, many of them American.[40] Davis remained there until August 1929, when he returned to New York. The studio was of a good size and well lit, with a sleeping balcony, an alcohol cooking stove, and a coal stove; one electric bulb provided nighttime illumination.[41]

Davis found himself in the midst of a lively literary and artistic milieu of Americans and international sophisticates. Elliot Paul, a writer friend from Gloucester days, showed him the sights when he first arrived. His neighbor Andrée Ruellan (half French and half American) gave parties and introduced

69. *Place Pasdeloup*

70. Cover for *transition*, no. 14

Fall 1928. Courtesy of The Harris
Collection of American Poetry and Plays,
Brown University, Providence, Rhode Island

Davis around. Rose and Robert Carlton Brown, his poet friend since *The Masses,*
arrived shortly after Davis. Alexander Calder lived nearby, as did Isamu
Noguchi and John Graham. The bohemian artist Jules Pascin attracted a following of young American artists, including George Biddle, Emil Ganso, and
Yasuo Kuniyoshi. Niles Spencer took Davis to see Hilaire Hiler, "who in turn

played the first Earl Hines record I ever heard."[42] During the day these convivial artists sat at the cafés, and in the evening they went to listen to jazz at such spots as the Jockey and the Bal Nègre.

In spite of all the distractions of Paris, Davis lost no time in plunging into work. Not only did he start several canvases, but he went to Edmond Desjobert's lithography atelier on the Rue d'Alésia. Other Americans who had worked at Desjobert's or were working there at the time included Louis Lozowick, Adolf Dehn, Yasuo Kuniyoshi, and Reginald Marsh.[43] During his Paris sojourn he did a total of ten lithographs of street scenes.

On September 17, 1928, just three months after arriving, Davis wrote a long letter to his father detailing his progress as an artist. He was fascinated by the physical environment of the ordinary Parisian: "I am principally interested in the streets. There is great variety, from the most commonplace to the unique. A street of the regular French working class houses of 100 years ago is always interesting because they are all different in regard to size, surface, number of windows etc."[44]

Even though ensconced in Paris, Davis had his eye on the New York art world. He sent an oil painting, two gouaches, and a lithograph of Paris street subjects to Edith Halpert for a "Paris by Americans" exhibition she was planning at the Downtown Gallery for that October. He was in good company in that exhibition; the other artists included Leon Kroll, Jules Pascin, Adolph Dehn, Yasuo Kuniyoshi, and Charles Locke.

Also in his letters to his mother and father Davis reported meeting the famous artists and patrons that drew young American artists to Paris. In that same lengthy September 17 letter he wrote:

I went to the studio of Fernand Léger, internationally famed modernist painter. He showed me all his newest work. Very strong. Next day he came to see my work. He liked the Egg Beaters very much and said they showed a concern of space similar to his latest development. Said it was interesting that 2 people who did not know each other should arrive at similar ideas. He thought the street scenes I am doing here too realistic for his taste but said they were drawn with fine feeling. He invited me to send something to a show he is organizing in January. I am going to Picasso's studio as soon as he comes back to town.[45]

And in November, he wrote to his mother: "Gertrude Stein came to see my paintings. She is the famous patron of Picasso. And I went to her place and saw all her Picassos and Gris paintings. I am going again tomorrow night. I think she will buy one [of] mine."[46] There being no evidence of such a purchase, we can assume that Stein did not after all buy a painting from Davis.

Elliot Paul gave Davis's career a boost when he featured the artist in the avant-garde magazine *transition*. Paul had been hired by Eugene Jolas, a Chicago newspaperman with European parents, to help launch the first issue, which appeared in February 1927 and included pieces by James Joyce, Kay Boyle, Gertrude Stein, Hart Crane, and Archibald MacLeish, among others.[47]

The streets of Paris proved to be endlessly fascinating to Davis, both for their historical associations and visual interest. On September 17, 1928, Davis wrote to his father about the Place des Vosges, "a small square surrounded by beautiful houses of Louis XIII design. . . . On one is a sign, Victor Hugo lived in this house from 1833 to 1843, on another is the sign, this was the city hall of the 8 district from 1790 to 1900, on another Marie Sevignée was born in this house in 1628 etc."

In spite of the historical associations of the site, he later denied such interests. In 1944, when the painting was exhibited at the Newark Museum, he wrote: "If one went to the Place des Vosges full of enthusiasm for its rich historical background, the fact that Victor Hugo lived there, etc., then the painting made to express that interest would have to be factual in the sense of being a color and shape replica of the Place des Vosges. But if one came accidentally into the Place des Vosges, unaware of its history, as I did, then the interest aroused comes purely from the physical aspect of the scene itself as it was displayed in the light of a certain kind of day. One paints this sort of interest without regard to historical accuracy, civic pride, or the name of the town or place. My picture looks like the Place des Vosges, but it looks only like certain color-shape relations which are inherently there. These color-shape relations are beautiful independently of the objects they are associated with."

When Davis visited him, Paul was no longer an assistant editor, but still helped to put out issues. His article "Stuart Davis, American Painter," along with four reproductions plus the cover illustration, appeared in the fall 1928 issue (see plate 70). Paul's praise is larded with half-truths and hyperbole: he asserts that Davis cut himself off from all American influences, that he drew "his inspiration from the genuine modern masters rejected by all his associates," and that "he has had no encouragement."[48] The characterization of Davis as the alienated expatriate might have made good copy, but it was far from the truth of the gregarious art enthusiast who never ceased giving credit to those who had encouraged and supported him.

In Paris, Davis did not neglect the café scene or the nightlife the city offered. On January 25, 1929, he wrote to his mother, using the stationery of the Café Bar Américain at 108 Boulevard du Montparnasse. The letter deserves to be quoted at length for its insight into the side of Paris that most impressed Davis:

Tonight we are going to the opening of Sandy Calders [sic] exhibit in the Rue de Boethe. . . . Nobody is much interested in his work but it is an excuse for a lot of people to bump into each other. There's no use talking, Paris is the place for artists. Here, an artist is accepted as a respectable member of the community whether he is good or bad. In the swellest cafés one can [sit] all afternoon with a 6¢ glass of coffee without anything being thought of it. At the next table people may be drinking champagne cocktails in dress suits. That is how it is different than N.Y. Clothes mean nothing; you can be well dressed or badly dressed nobody cares or pays any attention. Living is not much cheaper here than in N.Y. but if you are forced to and have good health you could live here on very little and still be around other people who are well to do.[49]

72. *Café, Place des Vosges*

In the evenings, Davis participated in the wild, bohemian parties that characterized American expatriate life. He was joined by Bessie Chosak, an American from Brooklyn. Bob Brown threw a party in Paris for the couple when they married. [50]

Another American artist in Paris, Ione Robinson, who attended classes with Noguchi and Andrée Ruellan, was horrified when she encountered Davis's bohemia. In a letter to her mother, dated September 20, 1928, she reported on one particular evening that left her feeling "too young for Europe." That night she met Jules Pascin, who "sat drinking glass after glass of a horrid green drink called pernod, yelling at everyone," and the Japanese artist Foujita, who "walks in his bare feet and wears earrings." The evening was capped by her introduction to Davis.

[He] took us all to a place where they said we would see African sculpture in the flesh, the Bal Nègre. I was so frightened at what I saw that I asked Mrs. Carroll to take me home. Mr. Davis asked me to dance, but it didn't work very well as he was trying to dance like the Negroes, who were as wild as anything I have ever seen. Mrs. Davis [Bessie Chosak] was wearing a hat of jet beads that made her head shine in the colored lights, and the Negro women, who come from French Martinique, wore large, bright-colored bandanas tied high on their heads. There were many Spahi troops in their red fezzes, dancing with many French girls. I felt so completely out of place that nothing anyone could say would make me stay at the Bal Nègre. Mr. Davis kept trying to persuade me that this was a wonderful experience, and the way to understand Negro sculpture, but I had had enough, and I finally got home.[51]

Later, in 1936, encountering Davis at a political meeting in New York, Robinson noted the difference between his 1930s social conscience and the time in 1928 when he had "no thought in his head . . . except painting squares and cubes."

Davis's paintings of Parisian street scenes did not advance the theoretical investigations of planes that he had begun in the Egg Beater series. As he explained in 1945 to Sweeney: "[I]n Paris, the actuality was so interesting I found a desire to paint it just as it was."[52] On the other hand, his street-scene paintings in no way imitate snapshots, nor do they emulate the picturesque scenes of Maurice Utrillo, well known in the 1920s for his Parisian views. While Davis tampers little with Parisian topography (see plates 68, 69), he does bring an inventiveness of color and textural variety to the works. He simplifies the planes and reduces the architectural embellishments, such as quoins and keystones, yet still retains a detail here and there to animate the composition and suggest locale. However, one innovation to his art stayed with him. It was in Paris that Davis first began to use the curving calligraphic line, at first to suggest smoke from a chimney (see *Rue Lipp,* plate 6), then, upon his return, to articulate an empty space (see *Interior,* plate 7), and finally "thickened" (see *The Paris Bit,* plate 117) to become a major element in his late painting.[53]

Letters to his parents through the winter and spring of 1929 include appeals for funds. Grateful for their help, he nevertheless decided to come home by the summer of 1929. Even though he was enjoying himself, the leisurely pace of artistic life was beginning to strike him as monotonous.[54] He never learned to speak the language well and he was, no doubt, eager to be back in the middle of the New York art scene. So, in August 1929, two months before the stock market crashed, Bessie and Stuart Davis sailed for home.

73. *Summer Landscape*

III. Political Protest and Social Theories of Art: The 1930s

LIKE MANY OTHER NEW YORK ARTISTS, Davis did not immediately feel the effects of the stock-market crash that fall of 1929; he was busy organizing his reentry into the New York art world. His first task upon his return from Europe was to secure an apartment for himself and his wife, Bessie, which he did at St. Luke's Place, Thirteenth Street and Seventh Avenue, not far from his parents' home in the Chelsea Hotel. Late in the summer he went on to Gloucester, while Bessie stayed in the city and worked at a drugstore owned by her brother.[1]

That fall Davis prepared to send pictures to exhibitions. He had a small show of nine watercolors at the Whitney Studio Galleries in November and December, consisting primarily of Gloucester scenes done that fall. During the run of the show he sold his gouache *New England Street* to Mrs. Force for 150 dollars, and three of his Paris lithographs for 15 dollars each. It might have been at this time that Davis gave Mrs. Force a Paris picture, *Place Pasdeloup* (plate 69), perhaps as compensation for the additional money she had sent him to extend his stay abroad.[2]

His dealer, Edith Halpert, welcomed him back with ideas for showing his work. She included four of his Paris lithographs in her "American Printmakers" exhibition at the Downtown Gallery the last two weeks of December. She also mounted a solo show of his recent work in late January 1930. The critics responded well to his thirteen oils of Paris street scenes. Lloyd Goodrich, writing for the February 1930 issue of *The Arts,* praised Davis for following the lead of Picasso, Léger, and Braque, and practicing an exacting abstract style, "admirably logical and consistent, and . . . engaging in its severe purity." However, Goodrich believed that the "language in which he has chosen to express himself seems unnecessarily limited," and wanted to see Davis develop further.[3] The critic for the *New York Post* thought "the third-dimensional suggestion of his design is subtly achieved by a highly personal use of spatial composition" and likened the paintings to musical compositions: "The paintings of these old corners of Paris do not suggest the actual character of these old haunts, filled with the ebb and flow of life, but are brilliant improvisations on such themes, using familiar notes and chords to produce quite an unfamiliar and highly modern melody."[4] It was the first time in print that a writer had linked Davis's compositions to musical scores; the analogy between pictures and music had long been used to explain modern art to the public and was to prove particularly apt for Davis's work in the following decades.

74. Photograph of the site of *Summer Landscape* in Gloucester

73. *Summer Landscape*

1930. Oil on canvas, 29 x 42"
The Museum of Modern Art, New York. Purchase

Davis sold Summer Landscape *to the Museum of Modern Art while he was strapped for funds during 1940. When Alfred H. Barr, Jr., director of the museum, wrote his influential book* What Is Modern Painting? *in 1943, he featured this work along with a snapshot of the scene (plate 74). To Barr, Davis had "transformed a prosaic, commonplace view into a lively, decorative composition." Barr explains, "How did he go about it? First he drew the forms in simple outlines, leaving out unimportant or confusing details and reducing board fences, clouds and ripples to a lively linear shorthand. By omitting all shadows he lets you see these essential shapes and patterns more clearly. He moves houses around. . . . But with all these omissions and simplifications and rearrangements Davis has given a clearer and more complete idea of the village than does the snapshot. . . . [He] has even caught the lighthearted spirit of a summer day."*

Davis himself published a defense of American modernism in the February 1930 issue of *Creative Art*. In a long open letter to Henry McBride, a critic who had been sympathetic to his work since the early 1920s, Davis took issue with McBride's judgment that this "swell American painter," as McBride called him, leaned too heavily on French Cubism for his style. Davis seized the opportunity to state his belief that art belonged to the world and that all artists learned from an international roster of advanced painters, just as scientists learned from the leaders in their fields; and, moreover, influences were good:

I did not spring into the world fully equipped to paint the kind of pictures I want to paint. It was therefore necessary to ask people for advice. This resulted in my attending the school of Robert Henri where I received encouragement and a vague idea of what it was all about. After leaving the direct influence of Mr. Henri I sought other sources of information and as the artists whose work I admired were not personally available I tried to find out what they were thinking about by looking at their pictures. Chief among those consulted were Aubrey Beardsley, Toulouse Lautrec, Fernand Léger and Picasso. . . . I admit the study and the influence and regard it as all to the good. But why one should be penalized for a Picasso influence and not for a Rembrandt or a Renoir influence I can't understand. . . . Picasso himself has as many influences as Carter has pills.[5]

With this statement, he was not only correcting Elliot Paul's article in *transition,* but firmly stating a belief in the collective nature of art making that he maintained throughout his life. Indeed, Davis always thrived among artists as intensely involved with art as he. His close friends in the years right after his return from Paris were John Graham and Arshile Gorky, artists also developing abstract compositions. It was Graham who mentioned Davis's Downtown Gallery show to Duncan Phillips, one of the few patrons actively buying art in the early 1930s.[6] And it was Gorky whom Davis corralled into writing an article on him for the September 1931 issue of *Creative Art,* when the editor of the magazine insisted that a second article accompany Davis's own "Self-Interview." Davis especially relished Gorky's flamboyance, strong opinions, and humor.[7] The friendships consolidated in the early 1930s; the younger artist Jacob Kainen later recalled that by 1934, Graham, Davis, and Gorky "were generally recognized by alert artists as the Magus figures in the New York art world."[8]

The big events of the 1929–30 and 1930–31 seasons were the exhibitions mounted by the recently opened Museum of Modern Art. The Modern's second show, and its first of contemporary art, "Paintings by Nineteen Living Americans," proved the catholicity of taste of its first director, Alfred H. Barr, Jr. Barr chose a range of artists, from the Whitney crowd to the Stieglitz circle—realist artists John Sloan, Edward Hopper, Rockwell Kent, Walt Kuhn, and Kenneth Hayes Miller, as well as the more abstract artists Charles Demuth, Lionel Feininger, Max Weber, and Georgia O'Keeffe. Davis, while not invited to that first show, was in good company when asked to participate in another, similar show, "Painting and Sculpture by Living Americans," which opened in December 1930; the

artists included William Glackens and George Luks from the old Henri group, and Arthur Dove, Guy Pène du Bois, Marsden Hartley, Charles Sheeler, William Zorach, and two of Davis's friends from Paris, Niles Spencer and Alexander Calder. His relationship with the Modern was one he would quite naturally cultivate, just as he had his relationships with Gertrude Vanderbilt Whitney and Juliana Force, who at that time had temporarily closed the Whitney Studio Galleries in preparation for the opening, in November 1931, of their latest enterprise—the Whitney Museum of American Art.

During 1930 and 1931, Davis returned to still lifes, Gloucester landscapes, New York street scenes, and a series, called New York/Paris, that combined motifs of the two cities. When his output from these years is spread out, a waxing and waning of influences can be observed as Davis feels his way toward his own unique style, one that he can support with a theoretical rationale.

75. *New York/Paris No. 2*

1931. Oil on canvas, 30 x 40"
Portland Museum of Art, Maine. Hamilton Easter
Field Art Foundation Collection, Gift of Barn
Gallery Associates, Inc., Ogunquit, Maine, 1979

76. *New York/Paris No. 1*

1931. Oil on canvas, 39 x 54¾"
The University of Iowa Museum of Art,
Iowa City. Museum Purchase

*In the five paintings of the New York/
Paris series, Davis seems less interested
in creating inventive spatial compositions than in laying out a decorative
design of motifs from his own paintings
of Paris and New York. The woman's
leg, however, seems to have been appropriated from a Man Ray photograph,
reproduced in the April 1921 issue of
New York Dada.*

77. *Radio Tubes*

1931. Oil on canvas, 50 x 32¼"
Rose Art Museum, Brandeis University, Waltham,
Massachusetts. Bequest of Louis Schapiro, Boston

With Radio Tubes, *Davis makes an iconic image by vertically centering the forms against a dense background of parallel horizontal lines suggestive of radio waves.*

78. *Egg Beater No. 5*

1930. Oil on canvas, 50⅛ x 32¼"
The Museum of Modern Art, New York.
Abby Aldrich Rockefeller Fund, 1945

One of Davis's first large still-life paintings upon his return from Paris, Egg Beater No. 5 might be considered an anomaly in his developing oeuvre, since it adheres much more closely to the forms of a real egg beater, guitar, vase, and table than did his earlier Egg Beater paintings. This most French of his still-life paintings brings to mind Miró's elegant, large Table with Glove of 1921 (The Museum of Modern Art, New York), but it does not indicate the direction that his art would take.

With some exceptions, the Gloucester landscapes from 1930 and 1931 have a more sparse quality than the Paris works. For one thing, he applies paint less thickly, rarely using the palette knife to achieve a textured impasto, and he creates open spaces around his forms. Of course, each place has its own character—Paris with its narrow streets and rows of adjoining Second Empire apartments and shops, and Gloucester with its schooner masts, harbors, and village centers. Davis took advantage of those differences and emphasized them. Hence, in the Gloucester landscapes, such as *Summer Landscape* (plate 73), buildings do not tightly overlap, unlike the Paris scenes, where our access to an open vista is blocked. For Gloucester, he suggests its airy openness by including patches of sky, squiggles of foliage, the masts of ships, and a space that stretches out into a background of smaller and smaller buildings.

In the area of still life, Davis also moved gradually away from the more solidly rendered *Egg Beater No. 5* (plate 78) to two large, handsome paintings, *Salt Shaker* (The Museum of Modern Art, New York) and *Radio Tubes* (plate 82), both painted in 1931. In these two latter paintings the forms are locked into the center of a band of painted lines. However, other paintings begun in 1930, such as *Interior* (plate 7) and *Still Life—Flowers* (plate 82), pointed him toward an openness of forms. These two contain parts of objects surrounded by large shapes of space. The space is indeterminate, much like the Surrealist space that Joan Miró developed in the late 1920s (see plate 81); moreover, the drawn lines within Davis's compositions thicken to hint at recognizable and often wittily fashioned forms but also serve to enliven the surface, again like Miró. Since the Valentine Gallery held an exhibition of that artist's paintings in 1930, Davis might well have been inspired by Miró's witty use of line.

In *Still Life—Flowers,* Davis includes an oversized, and very abstracted, vase of flowers perching precariously on a golf course (note the flag rising from the ninth hole); musical notes articulate a "leaf" and a directional arrow points to an outline drawing of a hotel facade. The suggestion of witty allusions (the flying pennants marked "H" and "Y" refer to Harvard and Yale), bright colors, clearly outlined forms, directional lines, squiggles and curls further remind one of Miró's playful Surrealist works.

But it was not solely influences from art that worked their way into Davis's paintings. During the early 1930s, as in previous decades, he roamed the New York streets making sketches of buildings, signs, bridges, and streetlights, just as he had hiked over East Gloucester making picture notes of boats, rigging, seagulls, piers, and nets. Some of the line drawings approximate the scene he would see before his eyes; other drawings are more inventive, combining and superimposing motifs to effect a lively pattern. But when he worked them up into finished pictures, such as *Jefferson Market* (plate 85), he did not hesitate to refer to earlier studies done in the 1920s (see plate 86).

When the New York/Paris scenes were shown at the Downtown Gallery in April 1931, Davis wrote in the catalogue concerning the ideas he was then formulating about art. His remarks served as his first public pronouncement (there had earlier been letters to critics and private notes in his journals) of his theories about abstract painting. They deserve to be quoted in full, after which we can analyze the points Davis makes:

> *These pictures are in part the result of the following ideas:*
> *That a picture must tell a story.*
> *This story can have pictorial existence only through the artist's concept of form. There are an infinite number of form concepts available.*
> *My own is very simple and is based on the assumption that space is continuous, and that matter is discontinuous. In my formal concept the question of two or more dimensions does not enter. I never ask the question, "Does this picture have depth or is it flat?"*

79. *Artist in Search of a Model*

1931. Gouache on paper, 11 x 19" (sight)
Private collection

Although Davis did not choose the direction of biomorphic Surrealism, he painted several small landscapes in 1931 that have Surrealist overtones — recognizable shapes, exaggerated and often ballooning, set within an almost convincing three-dimensional spatial composition. Both Artist in Search of a Model *and* Television *(plate 80) contain overlapping organic shapes as well as cartoonlike human forms or parts of a human form. In* Artist in Search of a Model, *several figures are included in a beach scene where most of them look at a stretched canvas; in* Television, *two figures sit on the edge of a painted frame and look at the landscape spread out before them as so many dashes and dots. Davis could rarely satisfactorily integrate the human figure into his scenes; when he did, they often seem to stand as if outside the space-form compositions looking in.*

I consider such a question irrelevant. I conceive of form (matter) as existing in space in terms of linear direction. It follows then that the forms of the subject are analyzed in terms of angular variation from successive bases of directional radiation.

The phenomena of color, size, shape, and texture are the result of such angular variation.

I wish to make clear that I do not employ any system of angular proportion. The directions chosen and the resultant form of the picture are arbitrary.

I believe that all possible forms are valid and that limitations resulting from a set ratio or angle or area are not helpful in the production of forms other than themselves.

In other words, that the concept of a certain type of design which is good, opposed to another which is bad, is the wrong way to think about it. Any design which achieves variety is good.

If it achieves a known variety it does not interest us.

If it achieves a known but still unanalyzed variety, it has value.

In my conception, the idea of a picture which has good color and bad drawing is a meaningless one.

It can have meaning only from the standpoint of the spectator selecting a drawing made by the color in part, as opposed to the entire drawing of the artist.

Color must be thought of as texture which automatically allows one to visualize it in terms of space.

Aside from this, it has no meaning.[9]

The words Davis chose to describe his thoughts about painting were not arbitrary, but had been thought out carefully and expressed in letters to Edith Halpert in the months before the exhibition. In his catalogue statement he makes four main points that distinguish him from many of the other semi-abstract painters then working in the United States and abroad.

First: A picture tells a story, but it does so through a selection of forms culled from infinite possibilities without regard to rules or systems. Davis felt it important, as he had ten years earlier, that pictures be based on twentieth-century experience and that the world of objects—whether older structures and artifacts or contemporary, technological forms and devices—was part of that experience.

Second: "Space is continuous." Whereas in *Radio Tubes* Davis attempted to obliterate fluid space by imposing parallel, painted stripes in the areas surrounding his vacuum-tube forms, he rarely pursued this tactic again. However, in many later pictures he did create such dense patterns of object and surrounding space (figure and ground) that the space and forms became locked together as tightly as jigsaw-puzzle pieces.

Third: "Matter is discontinuous." Objects in the real world are discrete things—separate from one another. A Renaissance master would give pictorial unity to a collection of things through directional lighting and chiaroscuro, while Davis wanted to solve the problem of the unity of objects in a more novel

80. *Television*

1931. Tempera on paper, 10½ x 18″
Private collection

81. Joan Miró, *Dutch Interior, I*

1928. Oil on canvas, 36⅛ x 28¾″
The Museum of Modern Art, New York.
Mrs. Simon Guggenheim Fund

82. *Still Life—Flowers*

1930. Oil on canvas, 40 x 32"
Collection New Trier High School,
Winnetka, Illinois

and modern way—what he called the Picasso-American way of form analysis, rather than the Rembrandt-American way of perspective and chiaroscuro. To this end he came to the original conclusion that discrete objects relate to each other by sharing common planes. He then developed pictures where the extension of one plane of an object, stopped by a spatial interval, could be seen to reappear as the surface of another object. In other words, there is a plane, a spatial stop, and then an extension of the original plane, as in, for example, *Landscape with Garage Lights* (plate 83).

Fourth: "The phenomena of color, size, shape, and texture are the result of such angular variation." Davis means that once the composition is set, the other qualities—color, size, shape, and texture—act to bring harmony or dissonance to the structural directions within the painting.

83. *Landscape with Garage Lights*

1932. Oil on canvas, 32 x 41⅞"
Memorial Art Gallery of the University of
Rochester. Marion Stratton Gould Fund

When Davis showed his New York and Gloucester paintings at the Downtown Gallery in March 1932, a reproduction of this painting graced the cover of the brochure. Edith Halpert, Davis's dealer, called the exhibition "The American Scene" as part of the concerted effort by dealers to encourage potential buyers to acquire American art during the Depression years.

Davis's reasoning, at times hard to follow, is purely pictorial, eschewing questions of emotional response. The way he plotted out his moves, like a chess master (he was in fact a superb chess player), was not unlike that of others who thought and wrote about "plastic form." This apt term denoted the preoccupation of artists and critics with the kinds of forms that suggest spatial illusionism—not mere flat, colored shapes placed here and there to articulate a surface. Although the problem to be solved was the classic one of translating three-dimensional nature to the flat surface of the canvas or paper, the solution that Davis and many other modernists strove for was to be elegant, like a mathematical equation, and witty. Above all, Davis seemed to want to depersonalize his art and give it a basis akin to science.

Early 1932 was particularly busy for Davis. In March he had a solo exhibition at the Downtown Gallery that featured new work, such as *House and Street* (plate 8), *Radio Tubes* (plate 77), *Landscape with Garage Lights* (plate 83), *Television* (plate 80), and *Jefferson Market* (plate 85). Davis must have cringed when he read Edward Alden Jewell's review for the *New York Times:* "[W]ith Stuart Davis everything is design. His bright, strong, flat colors are worked out in a scheme that at all points furthers the immediate design problem. . . . [T]he assembled shapes of color resemble cut-outs applied upon a plain surface."[10] While flat design was important to Davis, these remarks deny the considerable efforts he made to construct pictorial space through angular variation.

In February of that year Lincoln Kirstein began organizing an exhibition of mural studies at the Museum of Modern Art that would inaugurate the muse-

84. *New York Street Scene*

1926. Oil on panel, 24 x 16"
Columbus Museum of Art, Ohio.
Gift of Harry Spiro

um's new quarters at 11 West Fifty-third Street. He wrote to Davis, as well as to over three dozen painters and a dozen photographers, stating: "The Advisory Committee feels that mural painting in America has suffered from a lack of opportunity to assert itself. At the present time such an exhibition would be particularly valuable for the information of many interested architects in New York who are in search of competent decorators for buildings proposed or in construction."[11] Kirstein asked the artists to submit a horizontal panel measuring twenty-one by forty-eight inches of three scenes, and a larger, seven-by-four-foot panel based on one of the three scenes. The subject was to be "some aspect of the post-war world."

The exhibition was organized, in part, to placate artists furious that American painters had not been commissioned to decorate the walls of Rockefeller Center, then under construction. Ralph Pearson's New School students drew up a petition, and John Sloan, as president of the Art Students League, also wrote in protest. Many of the artists whom Kirstein wanted to win over to the exhibition project were the activist radicals of the John Reed Club, the artists' organization founded in 1929 by artists who were close to the Communist Party. Not

85. *Jefferson Market*

1930. Oil on canvas, 33¾ x 23"
Fayez Sarofim Collection, Houston

86. Sheet from Sketchbook 6

1926. Pencil on paper, 8½ x 6¾"
Collection Earl Davis, courtesy
Salander-O'Reilly Galleries, New York

surprisingly, these artists took the opportunity to submit panels critical of capitalism and celebrating workers' struggles; many had no intention of showcasing their skills as potential muralists. The politically charged paintings of William Gropper, Ben Shahn, Benjamin Kopman, and especially Hugo Gellert's painting called *Us Fellas Gotta Stick Together*—a caricature of J. P. Morgan, Henry Ford, and John D. Rockefeller, Sr., shown surrounded by bags of money as they huddle behind Al Capone and his machine gun—proved embarrassing to the museum's staff and trustees when the show opened in May 1932, and the whole exhibition came close to being cancelled.[12] Many of the other radical artists in the exhibition were more restrained in their art, such as Maurice Becker and Glenn Coleman, old friends of Davis's. They had regularly contributed to *New Masses,* the semi-independent journal issued by editors associated with the Communist Party. Davis himself had sent drawings to *New Masses* in the 1920s, but there is little evidence that in 1932 he had begun to align himself with the politics of the left.

Davis's own large, seven-foot panel for the mural show was called in the museum's catalogue *Abstract Vision of New York: A Building, a Derby Hat, a Tiger's*

87. Study for *New York Mural*

1932. Pencil on paper, 9 x 7¾"
Norton Museum of Art,
West Palm Beach, Florida.
Gift of Earl Davis

88. *New York Mural*

1932. Oil on canvas, 84 x 48"
Norton Museum of Art,
West Palm Beach, Florida

This seven-foot-high painting was inclu-
ded in the mural exhibition at the Muse-
um of Modern Art, New York, in 1932.

89. *T-Scape (T-View)*

1932 (repainted 1951). Oil on canvas, 21 x 14"
Hirshhorn Museum and Sculpture Garden,
Smithsonian Institution, Washington, D.C.
Gift of Joseph H. Hirshhorn, 1966

*This painting is the right panel of the
three-part study for* New York Mural.
*According to William Agee, Davis re-
painted the work in 1951, at which time
he retitled it* T-View. *Conservation reports at the Hirshhorn Museum indicate
that Davis repainted only the color and
did not tamper with the shapes.*

Head, and Other Symbols (plate 88), a title he later made a point of changing to
New York Mural since he abhorred the word "abstract" when applied to his paint-
ings. While neither this nor the smaller, three-part composition, called simply
Abstract Vision of New York (see plate 89 for the right side); could be considered
anticapitalist or controversial, it had political references within its imagery to
Democratic Party machine politics (Tammany tigers), Al Smith's unsuccessful

90. Study for
Men without Women

1932. Ink and pencil on paper, 11 x 17"
Private collection

91. Photograph of *Men without Women* installed at Radio City Music Hall, New York

bid for the presidency in 1928 (his brown derby and a banana—from "Yes, We Have No Bananas," the theme song of the Smith campaign), and the bootleg liquor of Prohibition (martini glass). Many of the critics deplored what they considered a "sorry show," but Davis's mural was singled out for praise by the critic for the *New York American*.[13]

June 1932 should have been a high point for Davis's career, but it was a sobering time for him personally. In mid-June his twenty-six-year-old wife, Bessie Chosak Davis, died from an infection following an abortion. The relationship between the two of them at that time is unclear, and they could well have been living separately at the time since the address given on her death certificate differs from Davis's residence during June 1932. Nevertheless, from all accounts, her death profoundly sorrowed him.[14] Fortunately, when he moved to Gloucester for the summer, he had a new project that would absorb him fully.

Edith Halpert had managed to land him a major commission: a mural for Radio City Music Hall, which was then under construction. The mural was to be installed in the spacious men's lounge designed by the interior decorator Donald Deskey (plate 91). Davis left New York for Gloucester, where he rented space in the Bradford building, and began working out the design problems. By November he had finished the eleven-by-seventeen-foot painting and shipped it down to New York.[15]

Appropriate to its site, the mural, *Men without Women,* celebrates male leisure with its motifs from the world of smoking and gambling, motoring and sailing, and barbershops. The title refers to Ernest Hemingway's collection of short stories published in 1927. Davis had originally suggested that it be done with pieces of cutout linoleum, a medium he had experimented with, but New York fire regulations prevented this.[16]

Davis could be called lucky to have the Radio City commission in 1932, even though he later complained that the pay was barely sufficient to support him. He had just lost his teaching job at the Art Students League because of cutbacks,[17] and paintings in his show that spring at the Downtown Gallery, while receiving praise in the press, did not sell well. Although he still had the monthly stipend of 50 dollars from Halpert, in exchange for his artwork, that had begun in October 1930, her payments were becoming more irregular due to the falling economy. In September 1932, Halpert wrote to Davis that she was pleased his stipend was working out for him, and she added: "I have no qualms about the sales as that will take care of itself in the future. If conditions had been different last year I am sure we should not have had to limit our payments as we did of late, and we should have been prepared to continue helping you financially and that you will continue doing the fine work you have done."[18] One year later, Halpert was no longer able to advance Davis funds, in spite of his pleas to her;[19] however, she did, at that time, renew her efforts to sell his paintings.

The Great Depression was deepening. Customers became reluctant to buy, and commercial galleries began to close. When the sixteenth annual exhibition of the Society of Independent Artists ended in April 1932, *Art Digest* reported that in lieu of sales, some forty to fifty pictures had been bartered away for goods and services—"everything from zoology lessons to 88 pounds of coffee"—compared to about ten sold for cash.[20] *Art Digest* also reported that Edgar J. Bernheimer, writing in the *New York Times,* had lamented: "Today, for all practical purposes, the private buyer has disappeared. There remains only the museums."[21] The museums responded in varying ways during 1932. The Metropoli-

92. *American Painting*

Original state, 1932. Oil on canvas, 40 x 50¼"
Photograph Collection Earl Davis

The state of American Painting *shown here was overpainted in 1942, worked on again in 1948, and reached its present state in 1951 (see plate 114). Another version,* Tropes de Teens *(plate 115), painted in 1956, completely eliminates the top-hatted figure and the hand with a pointed gun. Holliday Day, John Lane, and Lewis Kachur have teased interpretations from these successive images and their sequential changes. Lane sees the top-hatted figure as a Jiggs character from the comic strip "Bringing Up Father." Kachur notes that in gambling circles "Little Joe" refers to the number four on dice; the airplane was identified by Day as the Wedell-Williams Racer, a prize-winning plane in the early 1930s. Kachur suggests that the four figures represented Davis and his friends John Graham, Arshile Gorky, and either Jan Matulka or Willem de Kooning. When Davis revised the painting in 1951 he X'ed out the third figure, in reference to Gorky's death.*

tan Museum was stepping up its policy, *Art Digest* noted, of "purchasing paintings by contemporary artists from art dealers, thereby, in these times of stress, giving encouragement to both." The Whitney was going even further by purchasing art directly from artists; in May it announced a 20,000-dollar fund to purchase paintings from its first Biennial exhibition.[22]

Juliana Force invited Davis to submit a painting for that first Whitney Biennial. On October 5, 1932, he reported to Edith Halpert the invitation from the Whitney and said he would submit "a special painting" done from drawings he had on hand.[23] His entry, *American Painting* (plate 92), introduced motifs from an anticapitalist iconography then being developed by his radical artist friends from the show at the Museum of Modern Art. Most noticeable is the hand loosely holding a gun to the head of a gent in a top hat, a motif that signified capitalism. Other motifs, however, refer to popular culture. Unusual in Davis's oeuvre was the inclusion here of a complete sentence, a line from a Duke Ellington lyric: "It don't mean a thing, if it ain't got that swing." In hanging the exhibition, Force placed this work in the stairwell, prompting Davis to conclude that she was less than satisfied with the painting.[24]

In the spring of 1933, Davis started up a class in his place at Fourteenth Street and Eighth Avenue. He later explained to Harlan Phillips that he found this teaching so exhausting that when the students left, at one in the afternoon, he went out to McSorley's Saloon or Romany Marie's coffeehouse and then to a speakeasy on Christopher Street before returning home at two the next morning. This routine lasted until June, at which point he left for Gloucester to stay with his family because he no longer could afford the rent.[25]

That September he wrote to Halpert that he was "stranded in Gloucester," and could she send him funds.[26] She could not, but she did put him in touch with Sam Kootz, later one of the major dealers for the Abstract Expressionists, who had then undertaken a project to commission artists as designers of textiles. Kootz paid Davis 40 dollars for some designs which were later made into fabric (see plate 100). Kootz also bought two paintings from Halpert, providing Davis with more funds.[27] Davis finally left Gloucester on Christmas Day, 1933, returning to New York to a room at Romany Marie's at Eighth Street and MacDougal. In the next months he lived in several places in the Village, including his brother's apartment.

Thus, when the Public Works of Art Project started up, in December 1933, with Juliana Force as the New York director, Davis was there on the spot to become one of the first to sign up. The 34-dollar average weekly salary allowed him to make ends meet for several months, until he was discharged at the end of April. Controversies beset such a relief program for artists. The radical artists argued that artists in need should be hired, while Force and Edward Bruce, who had set up the program in Washington, insisted on artistic merit as the major employment criterion. Nevertheless, the P.W.A.P. showed what government could do for artists by providing them with regular paychecks for their artwork. The P.W.A.P. was followed a year later by the Federal Art Project, created in August 1935, which by October had come under the organizational control of the Works Progress Administration.[28]

In the meantime, as conditions for artists worsened, Davis, following Ben Shahn, Philip Evergood, and others, gravitated to left politics and to activist artists' organizations. The month Davis returned to New York, in December 1933, he contributed a work to a benefit exhibition and sale on behalf of the *New Masses* and also joined the John Reed Club.[29] The next February, he participated in the protests called by Hugo Gellert and others on the Artists Committee for Action that were mounted against the destruction of Diego Rivera's mural at Rockefeller Center.[30] Davis had also joined the American Society of Painters, Sculptors, and Gravers, a group whose members refused to participate in the "First Municipal Art Exhibition" that month because it was being held in a gallery in the same R.C.A. Building of Rockefeller Center where the destruction had taken place. But by far the most effective organization was the Artists Union, which grew out of the Emergency Work Bureau Artists Group, a small band of militant John Reed Club artists who were agitating for jobs, and which soared to 1,700 members when the federal government began hiring artists in fall 1935. Davis, the vice president of the organization in 1935, and other members became serious about trade-union solidarity.[31]

The year between mid-1934, when the P.W.A.P. folded, and August 1935, when the Federal Art Project started up, was a tough time to be a destitute artist. Henry McBride, when he reviewed the Davis show of Gloucester paintings held at the Downtown Gallery in April and May 1934, commented that both Davis and John Marin were modernists who were critically acclaimed but who lacked

93. Photograph of Stuart
Davis and Roselle Springer
at May Day March, 1935

sales. "So, since the Government is not yet actively committed to art and the aristocratic patron has vanished entirely, the only hope remaining to Mr. Davis is to appeal to the consciences of the museum directors throughout the land."[32] Davis followed this advice, but with mixed results.

By his own account, Davis's financial affairs hit rock bottom in the spring and summer of 1934, in spite of Edith Halpert's efforts to promote his pictures. Davis got in touch with the Baroness Hilla Rebay von Ehrenwiesen, who, with Solomon Guggenheim, was then assembling a collection that would become the nucleus of the Guggenheim Museum. In response, the Baroness agreed to see some of Davis's paintings in her Plaza Hotel suite. As Davis explained later, one of his watercolors "seemed to be non objective enough for her, providing I would fix it, meaning change it, so that—you know, that's the final insult. But I was in no position to object. I would have crawled in on my hands and knees, if necessary, because I needed the money, and that was the only place where I saw any possibility of getting any." So Davis "fixed it," the Baroness approved, and she sent him a check "for some pitiful amount." Even in the last years of his life the memory of the incident still rankled him.[33]

With Davis's commitment to radical politics deepening, the Baroness Rebay experience soured him even more on the private patronage system. When he spoke out against patronage and dealers in his August 28, 1935, article for the *American Magazine of Art,* "The Artist Today: The Standpoint of the Artists Union," his relations with his own dealer became strained. Halpert finally broke with him in early 1936.[34] Thus the 1934 show Davis had at the Downtown Gallery was to be his last solo exhibition anywhere until the early 1940s.

Although Davis had turned to the radical left as early as December 1933, he liked to dramatize his conversion as if it were a moment of epiphany. To Harlan Phillips he recalled:

I remember that I got out of bed on May Day when they used to have a May Day parade. I never thought of the May Day parade, or any other parade so far as that goes, but it was right in front of the house. I came down about noontime in a stupor out of bed, and here was this tremendous parade going on. That must have been in 1934 and then the next year I was marching in it. It wasn't a choice. It was a necessity to be involved in what was going on, and since it had a specific artist section connected with it—I mean it may have happened before to a lesser degree, but for the first time I know of, the artists felt themselves part of everything else, general depression, the needs of money and food and everything else.[35]

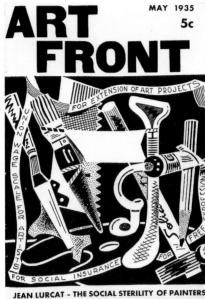

94. Cover of *Art Front*

May 1935. Courtesy Archives of American Art, Smithsonian Institution, Washington, D. C.

During 1934, 1935, and 1936, Davis plunged into activist art organizations protesting cutbacks of the government programs for the arts, boycotting policies that smacked of fascism, and issuing statements of solidarity with the Spanish republicans fighting Generalissimo Franco. Some friends, such as Gorky, dropped away from his political orbit. But during demonstrations or at meetings, frequently held in his own quarters on Seventh Avenue, he developed new friendships, including one with his future wife, the sculptor Roselle Springer.

His first important assignment in the radical artists' movement was as editor-in-chief of *Art Front,* a job he took over for its second issue, published in January 1935. He served as editor until February 1936, his eighth issue, when personality conflicts on the editorial board plus his own time commitments to the American Artists Congress made continued service problematical.[36] The first number of *Art Front* reported on current issues such as the union's job actions and the efforts of the Artists Committee for Action to establish an artist-run municipal art gallery and center. With the second number, Davis and the editorial board expanded the magazine to include a book review and art reviews. *Art Front* soon established a reputation as the liveliest art journal coming out of New York. Davis seemed to be tireless—in touch with a network of hundreds of artists, persuading notable critics such as Meyer Schapiro to write for the magazine,[37] writing polemical essays himself, scrapping with art critics, hectoring museum directors about rental fees for artists, and lecturing on the social need for art.

Davis encouraged a range of political viewpoints within the left perspective. Artists' styles were hotly debated. For example, for the January 1935 issue Davis wrote a review praising the Salvador Dali paintings at the Julien Levy Gallery. Conceding the conventional aspects of Dali's painting, Davis nevertheless liked his "fantastic visual juxtapositions" and concluded that "his ability to isolate and give concrete form to the associational aspects of a subject is unparalleled."[38] In the next issue, Clarence Weinstock, another *Art Front* staff member, vigorously disagreed and called Dali a "sophisticated illustrator" whose paintings were reactionary.

One enemy was common to all *Art Front* artists, writers, and editors: the American Regionalists—particularly Thomas Hart Benton, Grant Wood, and John Steuart Curry—who had been trumpeted by *Time* magazine in 1934 as "destined to turn the tide of artistic taste in the United States."[39] Davis went on

95. *Sixth Avenue El*

1931. Lithograph, 11⅞ x 17¼"
Whitney Museum of American Art,
New York. Purchase, with funds from
Mr. and Mrs. Samuel M. Kootz, 77.74

96. *Composition*

1935. Oil on canvas, 22¼ x 30⅛"
National Museum of American Art,
Smithsonian Institution, Washington, D.C.

the attack with his article "The New York American Scene in Art," published in the February 1935 *Art Front.* Of Benton, Davis questioned: "Are the gross caricatures of Negroes by Benton to be passed off as 'direct representation'? The only thing they directly represent is a third-rate vaudeville character cliché with the humor omitted. Had they a little more wit, they would automatically take their place in the body of propaganda which is constantly being utilized to disfranchise the Negro politically, socially and economically." Against Curry, Davis made another rhetorical sally: "How can a man who paints as though no laboratory work had ever been done in painting, who willfully or through ignorance ignores the discoveries of Monet, Seurat, Cézanne and Picasso and proceeds as though painting were a jolly lark for amateurs, to be exhibited in county fairs, how can a man with this mental attitude be considered an asset to the development of American painting?" Davis also attacked the critic Thomas Craven, who promoted the Regionalists, for his "vicious and windy chauvinistic ballyhoo."[40] Benton and Curry were miffed, and they were allotted space for rejoinders in the April 1935 issue.

Meanwhile, Davis had been asked to write the introduction to the catalogue of the exhibition "Abstract American Painting," held at the Whitney Museum in February and March 1935. In his brief essay, further cut down by the museum's staff, Davis points to the Armory Show of 1913 as marking the point when "the American artist became conscious of abstract art." As to the definition of abstract art, that varies with each individual artist: "This is so because the generative idea of abstract art is alive. It changes, moves and grows like any other living organism. However, from the various individual answers some basic concordance could doubtless be abstracted." To Davis, art should not pretend to be a copy of nature:

Art is not and never was a mirror reflection of nature. All efforts at imitation of nature are foredoomed to failure. Art is an understanding and interpretation of nature in various media. . . . Our pictures will be expressions which are parallel to nature and parallel lines never meet. We will never try to copy the uncopyable but will seek to establish a material tangibility in our medium which will be a permanent record of an idea or emotion inspired by nature. This being so, we will never again ask the question of painting, "Is it a good likeness, does it look like the thing it is supposed to represent?"

For him, art expresses the experiences an artist has, and it has its own reality: "Instead we will ask the question, 'Does this painting which is a defined two-dimensional surface convey to me a direct emotional or ideological stimulus?' . . . I believe that even in those cases where the artistic approach has been almost entirely emotional, the concept of the autonomous existence of the canvas as a reality which is parallel to nature has been recognized."[41] The clarity of Davis's comments no doubt found an appreciative audience among the general public who came to the Whitney's show.

Clarence Weinstock, however, attacked abstract art in the April 1935 issue of *Art Front*. To him abstract art was "founded on a limited definition of painting. . . . Form becomes like so much monopoly capital in which the society of art is sacrificed."[42] When Davis responded, he adopted the dialectical materialist approach that formed the basis of Weinstock's criticism and admitted that "Maybe the use of the phrase 'parallel to nature' is incorrect from the standpoint of philosophical usage. But the definition was meant to be a description of the material quality of a painting and did not by intention imply that because the painting was a quality distinct from its sources, it had no connection with them. Further, it did not by intention imply that the two-dimensional space definition was an act undirected by social purpose." To show that he does, in fact, understand dialectical materialism, he chastises Weinstock as "undialectical in his tendency to deny the reality of bourgeois origins and concomitants." Davis then goes on to say: "In the materialism of abstract art in general, is implicit a negation of many ideals dear to the bourgeois heart."

At the end of his essay in *Art Front* Davis includes the parts that were cut from the Whitney essay, namely, his assessment of the three tendencies in American painting that had developed since the late 1920s: first, the tendency toward cultural nationalism, that is, to be specifically "American" in one's art; second, the Surrealist direction; and third, "the necessity of a social content in art." He then argues for the necessity for the abstract artist to express social issues: "If the historical process is forcing the artist to relinquish his individualistic isolation and come into the arena of life problems, it may be the abstract artist who is best equipped to give vital artistic expression to such problems—because he has already learned to abandon the ivory tower in his objective approach to his materials."[43]

The ideas for Davis's essay for the Whitney catalogue and his *Art Front* postscript were percolating in the private notes that he typed for himself or entered into journals during the 1930s. These carefully dated entries reveal his struggles to synthesize his radical, Marxist political views with his ongoing project to develop an art theory for the modern age. Dialectical thinking helped him to work through the issues—on the one hand, to be realistic about the nature of space-color compositions, and, on the other, to recognize the class nature of art. An example comes from his notes of October 1, 1935:

The refusal to accept social purpose as primary in all human activity is, at best, unconscious insincerity. Thus, it becomes essential to day for the artist to think clearly in his life ideology as well as in his chosen medium. The human race, the workers, have arrived at that degree of development where conscious and scientific thought for their social direction must take the place of superstition and traditions. One either [has] a clear or a confused viewpoint with regard to social problems—and all special work in the Arts etc. is directed, not as an end in itself, but toward a social function, progressive or reactionary.

Davis ends this passage with a critique of "pure art" that cuts through the debates then raging in Marxist circles: "Arguments for pure art simply mean arguments for the perpetuation of the status quo, because in the artificial and unreal isolation of the artist's function implied in this concept, is implicit a refusal to admit the dynamic and moving quality of life. It is an undialectical and static concept placing itself in absolutes. It is a slave psychology because the artists feel that world events are beyond any power of theirs to change."[44]

The arguments within the offices of *Art Front,* at meetings of the Artists Union, and later of the American Artists Congress honed his ideas. During 1937, in particular, he wrote frequently in his journal as he worked out an original aesthetics for the modern artist that would dovetail artistic form and social

97. *The Terminal*

1937. Oil on canvas, 30⅛ x 40⅛"
Hirshhorn Museum and Sculpture Garden,
Smithsonian Institution, Washington, D.C.
Gift of Joseph H. Hirshhorn, 1966

content. Since Davis was then on the lecture circuit of leftist organizations, there is no doubt that he was simultaneously testing out these theories with an audience. He was critical of almost all previous approaches. Although he himself tended toward a dialectical materialist approach, he vigorously argued against the theories of Meyer Schapiro, then considered the leading Marxist critic. He felt Schapiro's Marxism was mechanistic, not giving enough weight to the active and positive role of artists in society.[45]

In April 1935, Davis began meeting with other politically active artists and cultural figures to discuss a new organization, less sectarian than the John Reed Club, that would appeal to liberal and centrist artists who themselves wanted to join the struggle against the spread of fascism and war preparations in Europe. This desire to create a large, broad-based alliance of artists came directly out of the Communist Party's policy change known as the Popular Front. The strategy meant that the Party would back away from its call for revolution against the capitalists and instead seek to forge alliances with "progressive" elements of the middle class in the fight against worldwide fascism. The immediate goal of

98. *Artists Against War
and Fascism*

1936. Gouache on paper, 12 x 16"
Fayez Sarofim Collection, Houston

Davis's group was to organize an American Artists Congress for two days in
February 1936, modeled on the successful American Writers Congress of April
1935. A call was sent out to artists; major figures in the cultural world, such as
Lewis Mumford and Meyer Schapiro, were invited to speak. The long-range purpose of the organization was "to achieve unity of action among artists of recognized standing in their profession on all issues which concern their economic
and cultural security and freedom, and to fight War, Fascism and Reaction,
destroyers of art and culture."[46]

For the next four years Davis steered the affairs of the American Artists
Congress, first as its executive secretary and later as national chairman. Other
board members included Max Weber, Louis Lozowick, Hugo Gellert, Yasuo
Kuniyoshi, and Philip Evergood. The Congress mounted large exhibitions and
produced traveling shows; sponsored lectures and symposia; pressed congress-
men for a permanent Bureau of Fine Arts; continued to hector museums to pay
rental fees to artists when they exhibited their work; and joined with other
groups in advancing legislation favorable to the growth of the arts in America.
It watched government projects closely to make certain that "standards" would
not be capriciously applied to eliminate needy artists. Davis carried on volumi-
nous correspondence regarding all such issues.

When the Federal Art Project started up in August 1935, Davis's friend Holger Cahill was asked to assume the responsibilities of national director. Cahill
had done publicity for the Independents shows, had curated exhibitions for
Edith Halpert, and was well known in the art community. He and his first wife
had been close friends with Dolly and John Sloan; with Davis he shared a pas-

sion for collecting jazz records. According to Davis, Cahill called on him to help decide about the offer. Davis described their momentous exchange while they were sitting in the backyard of a saloon made famous for its nighttime caterwauling cats: "He asked, 'Well, what do you think? It's a hell of a big job. I don't know whether I'm up to it.'. . . He was closer to the artists in their living and their problems than any other person, so you know, I said, 'For God's sake, take it! You'll be the savior of the whole situation.' "[47]

Cahill took the Washington job of heading up the Federal Art Project, and Audrey McMahon became the New York director. She was a tough administrator and had experience, since she had helped organize the relief program of the College Art Association in the early 1930s. Cahill, as a confirmed follower of the ideas of John Dewey, believed that art was a process, an activity that should be encouraged, and he defended the mandate that the F.A.P. take care of needy artists. His views contrasted with Edward Bruce, whose Treasury Section hired artists on the basis of their artistic merit. At the height of the project, the W.P.A. employed some five thousand artists nationwide in addition to models, art center staffs, and artists' assistants. Salaries varied by region, but generally senior artists were paid between 23 and 26 dollars a week, apprentices and models somewhat less. But the importance of the program was in providing artists with a steady income and with needed studios.

Cahill spelled out his philosophy in his introduction to the catalogue *New Horizons in American Art,* for the W.P.A. exhibition held at the Museum of Modern Art that showcased project artists. He took the occasion to reaffirm that "the Project has proceeded on the principle that it is not the solitary genius but a sound general movement which maintains art as a vital, functioning part of any cultural scheme." Cahill did not disagree that some artists were more talented than others, but he maintained that the memorable artworks of history were produced by artists who were "stimulated to creative endeavor" by an art movement.[48] His views paralleled those that Davis was expressing in his notebooks in the mid-1930s.

99. Study for *History of Communications*

1939. Ink on paper, 9⅝ x 29⅞"
Minnesota Museum of American Art,
St. Paul. Acquisition Fund Purchase, 80.08.1

100. *Textile with Liquor and Prohibition Motifs*

c. 1938 from design of 1934. Printed linen
The Brooklyn Museum, New York.
Gift of Mrs. Stuart Davis

As a penniless artist, Davis qualified for F.A.P. employment and was soon planning designs for murals under the program. Burgoyne Diller, supervisor of the mural division in New York City and an established abstract artist himself, assigned Davis to execute murals for the Williamsburg Housing Project, a twenty-building complex then being built by the F.A.P. and the New York Housing Authority. Twelve abstract artists were selected to paint murals for the social rooms and public areas. Reporting on the abstract murals of the W.P.A. for Holger Cahill, Diller remarked:

The decision to place abstract murals in these rooms was made because these areas were intended to provide a place of relaxation and entertainment for the tenants. The more arbitrary color, possible when not determined by the description of objects, enables the artist to place an emphasis on its psychological potential to stimulate relaxation. The

101. *Swing Landscape*

1938. Oil on canvas, 7 x 14'
Indiana University Art Museum, Bloomington

Davis painted Swing Landscape *for the Williamsburg Housing Project in Brooklyn, but it was never installed there. Instead, it was brought to Manhattan, where it hung in the Federal Art Gallery on Fifty-seventh Street. As the projects were being phased out in the early 1940s, the mural joined a two-person exhibition in Cincinnati; at that time Henry Hope purchased it for the Indiana University Art Museum in Bloomington.*

arbitrary use of shapes provides an opportunity to create colorful patterns clearly related to the interior architecture and complementing the architect's intentions.[49]

It was for the Williamsburg project that Davis executed *Swing Landscape* (plate 101). Drawing on the imagery of waterfront scenes of Gloucester, which he continued to visit during the summer months, he began work in 1936. Back in New York he worked with the help of two assistants in a studio on the sixth floor of the Art Project office at 235 East Forty-second Street.

In June 1937, however, he had a disagreement with Diller, who came to the studio to say that he wanted to transfer one of the assistants assigned to him. Davis protested that he needed that particular assistant to carry on "research"; Diller countered with the argument that Davis, as an abstract artist, did not need to do research. After Diller left, Davis was so angered by the incident that he

Davis frequently made notes to himself concerning his paintings. Of the WNYC mural, he wrote: "It represents a series of formal relations which are identified with musical instruments, radio antenna, ether waves, operators panel, electrical symbols, etc. These various elements are presented in an imaginative rather than a factual relationship. It has been my intention to place these various elements into juxtaposition with each other in a way which one often does in remembering a scene or event and the incidents relating to it. In remembering a scene, for example, certain aspects of it are exaggerated and others are suppressed. The scene is rearranged and recomposed according to the importance and meaning which the different elements have had for the spectator. This process of ideological composition is a common experience with everyone. The artist always does it in creating his pictures. In other words we do not simply reflect the things we see, like a mirror, but we compare them, in our ideas and emotions, with things we have seen before and with things we hope to see. This is what I have done in my mural. I have taken elements relating to radio and composed them in a harmonious design of shape, color, and direction. The result is a visual decoration which creates a mood in the spectator, just as a piece of music creates a mood, instead of giving some kind of factual information or instruction."

typed up a two-page memorandum spelling out his rationale for research, but whether the document found its way to a bureaucrat's desk is unknown.[50] However, we learn from the incident that Davis believed strongly that pictures were not made of arbitrary shapes and colors; the forms always came from the real world of urban objects and cultural artifacts, even though the shapes and colors were carefully orchestrated from his theories of space-composition.

With a steady income from his W.P.A. job, Davis married Roselle Springer in February 1938.[51] Her income as a secretary helped the couple's finances. Other assignments came to him, even though he was still actively engaged in running the American Artists Congress. He painted a project mural for New York City's Municipal Broadcasting Corporation, known as Studio B of WNYC (plate 102), and he also made color prints for the Graphic Arts Division. In 1939, he was again hired by the designer Donald Deskey, this time to paint *History of Communications* (see study, plate 99), a mural installed in the Hall of Communications at the New York World's Fair of 1939–40.

As the decade closed, the world situation had become tense, particularly after Hitler marched into Poland on September 1, 1939, only days after the Nazis had made a nonaggression pact with the Soviet Union. The conflicts were reflected in the internal struggles of the American Artists Congress, which Davis tried to hold together by keeping at bay attempts to politicize the organization. Since its founding in 1935, the Congress aimed to be a broad-based alliance of communists, socialists, and liberals. When the Soviet Union invaded Finland in December 1939, those in the organization opposed to the Communist Party proposed that the membership support Herbert Hoover's Finnish Relief Committee, which had been set up to assist the war victims there. The communists and their supporters in the organization argued that Hoover's committee was an anti-Soviet propaganda ploy, and they justified Stalin's invasion on the grounds that the defeated Finnish government was pro-fascist, with a history of massacring thousands of Finnish communists, and that valid principles of military defense had forced the Soviet Union to create a buffer against the Nazis.[52] In the debate at A.A.C. meetings, the majority backed the position that the A.A.C. should remain neutral on the Finnish question. However, a group of dissidents circulated a statement that the A.A.C. should "make clear to the world whether the Congress is a remnant of the cultural front of the Communist Party or an independent artists' organization." Bitter arguments ensued at meetings in April 1940. In the end, many resigned. With the organization now politicized, Davis also resigned.[53] His resignation marked the end of his political involvement in organizations.

But as he turned away from collective endeavors, new difficulties loomed ahead for him. Cut from the projects in the summer of 1939 and with few prospects, he was again pinched for funds. In the early 1940s, he was compelled to approach museum patrons and to make amends with his old dealer, Edith Halpert, in order to get on with his life of making art.

102. *Mural for Studio B, WNYC, Municipal Broadcasting Company*

103. *Report from Rockport*

IV. Hot and Cool Abstraction: The 1940s to the 1960s

IN FEBRUARY 1941, *Art News* PUBLISHED AN ARTICLE by Davis in which he declared his enjoyment of the "dynamic American scene" and asserted that all of his pictures had "their originating impulse in the impact of the contemporary American environment." He then went on to list "the things which have made me want to paint":

American wood and iron work of the past; Civil War and skyscraper architecture; the brilliant colors on gasoline stations; chain-store fronts, and taxi-cabs; the music of Bach; synthetic chemistry; the poetry of Rimbaud; fast travel by train, auto, and aeroplane which brought new and multiple perspectives; electric signs; the landscape and boats of Gloucester, Mass.; 5 & 10 cent store kitchen utensils; movies and radio; Earl Hines hot piano and Negro jazz music in general, etc.[1]

His list of typical things the artist would encounter in the American environment recalls the list R. J. Coady had set out as "American Art" in his first issue of *The Soil* in 1916 (see the Introduction). But, typical of Davis, he also acknowledged international culture, such as the music of Johann Sebastian Bach and the poetry of Arthur Rimbaud, as inseparable from the other influences. Having removed himself from the radical political scene in early 1940, he now had the time to concentrate on making art out of that "dynamic American scene."

His finances, however, were still precarious. On September 13, 1939, he spelled out his economic woes in a letter to Juliana Force, who as director of the Whitney Museum now made decisions independent of Mrs. Whitney. Davis explained that he had lost his job on the W.P.A. (because of regulations that called for the automatic curtailment of artists after eighteen months of employment); he was experiencing delays in getting back on; and he wanted to rent a studio that had become available in his building in order to start an art class in modern composition. Would the Whitney Museum consider purchasing some of his new work, he asked. Two days later he wrote to Duncan Phillips of Washington, D.C., describing his situation in more dire terms. He assured Phillips that a friend had offered to pay shipping and insurance costs for two pictures; would Phillips be interested in purchasing them? It took Mrs. Force about four weeks to reply that the Whitney had no purchase funds even though she might like to see his latest work. Phillips, on the other hand, replied immediately and sent Davis 400 dollars while he mulled over his choices.

In the meantime, Davis secured the studio and assured Phillips in a letter

104. *Town Square*

1925–26. Watercolor on paper, 11⅝ x 14½"
The Newark Museum, New Jersey. Purchase, 1936

In his 1960 book on Davis, Rudi Blesh called Town Square *and similar works the "empty stage paintings": "There are wings at either side, the regulation sort of rectangular flats upon which buildings are lightly sketched. Two trees at right center are cutout silhouettes that rest flatly on the floor and are abruptly cut off at the top where they would disappear in the flies. The terrain is not earth at all but a floor that recedes to the single vanishing point with which any theater-goer is familiar. Finally, there is the backdrop upon which are painted a garage and the sky. In the absence of any human beings the gasoline pumps exude that mysterious feeling of life that theatrical props assume on an empty-stage." He continued, "The empty stage, however, is the portent of action." Indeed, such empty stages as* Town Square *need only the viewer to activate them by imaginatively plunging into the streets.*

103. *Report from Rockport*

1940. Oil on canvas, 24 x 30"
The Metropolitan Museum of Art, New York.
Edith and Milton Lowenthal Collection,
Bequest of Edith Abrahamson Lowenthal, 1991

105. *Ana*

1941. Gouache on paper, 15⅝ x 15½"
Collection Mrs. Max Ellenberg

of December 15, 1939: "The studio I am now occupying, which your purchase made possible, is really wonderful. It is the first time I have been able to work outside my bedroom for 6 years. . . . I have made one advertising drawing and am trying to line up a few select students." In this letter he also mentions that he has written to the Metropolitan, the Whitney, and the Museum of Modern Art, "but for some strange reason none of them were interested."[2]

Years later he related the story to Harlan Phillips (no relation to Duncan) that the studio was actually another apartment across the hall from the one-room place he and Roselle were then living in; by taking it, he would then have the entire top floor of his building and would get two bathrooms to boot. Davis also confessed to Harlan Phillips (which he apparently did not mention to Duncan Phillips) that the landlord let him have the new place rent free for eight months.[3] Also, in spite of the plans he outlined to Duncan Phillips, there is no evidence that Davis took on any private students at this time. The fact was that he and Roselle needed money to live, but to confess such mundane realities, including the deal he had made with his landlord, would have seemed unprofessional.

Just before he received his second check from Phillips, Davis hatched a second money-making scheme which he proposed to Juliana Force in a letter of March 22, 1940. Would the Whitney consider publishing a book on the topic "Abstract Art in America Today," which he planned to write.[4] Force again declined. Seven months later, on October 29, he wrote again to urge her to buy one of his paintings. He offered reasons for such a sale: first, that the Whitney had not bought any of his work for ten years; and, second, since both the Museum of Modern Art and the Phillips Collection had purchased paintings within the year, he wanted "to be able to tell people that the Whitney Museum was still interested enough in my work to have made a current purchase." This time Force responded immediately, but as in her previous letters, she pleaded hard times for the Whitney, which had been forced to reduce its staff. Moreover, if she had money she felt obliged to "consider some of the artists who are not as yet represented" in the Whitney's collection. But she was at least sympathetic, and in early January 1941 came through for Davis by purchasing *House and Street* for 500 dollars. The artist responded with gratitude on January 18; however, he could not resist using the occasion to press Force to consider his murals.[5]

The sale helped him through the next months, but by midsummer he was desperate again. On July 14, 1941, he wrote a two-page letter to Elizabeth Sharkey, the executive secretary to Force, asking her to intercede on his behalf with the Whitney Museum. His "desperate situation," he confessed, prompted his "disagreeable and out-of-season appeal." He was not ashamed to present his predicament in detail. Davis assured Mrs. Sharkey that he had lined up lectures and a teaching position at the New School for the fall, but he needed funds to

106. *Arboretum by Flashbulb*

1942. Oil on canvas, 18 x 36"
The Metropolitan Museum of Art, New York.
Edith and Milton Lowenthal Collection,
Bequest of Edith Abrahamson Lowenthal, 1991

In a letter to the editor published in the New York Times, *September 27, 1942, Davis reiterated his stand that his work was not "abstract": "The 'Arboretum' was drawn from nature in a garden which I loved. The picture is an objective record of many of the forms and perspectives which were present there, for any one interested enough to have looked at them. But that is not all, because I have integrated in this interest many other observations, remote in time and place, with the general content, which was based on the initial interest felt in the color-space of the garden. The total result is a coherent dimensional statement, in terms of the three-dimensional color-space of painting, which has direct reference to the color-spaces, forms and tactile sensations we perceive in the world around us." The painting was favorably reviewed by the critics, and received honorable mention in 1944 at the Carnegie Institute's International Exhibition.*

107. *For Internal Use Only*

1944–45. Oil on canvas, 45 x 28″
Private collection

John Lane has brought to light the references in For Internal Use Only *to Piet Mondrian, the expatriate Dutch painter who lived in New York during World War II. Lane, when organizing the large Davis retrospective in 1978, spoke to the original owner of the painting, Mrs. Burton Tremaine. She recalled for Lane that she had discussed the work with Davis, who said that "the title had to do with his recollections of Mondrian and how he missed their experiences listening to jazz together. Davis pointed out that the picture contained the abstracted piano keys, bow tie, and black face of one of Mondrian's favorite boogie-woogie pianists, and the abstracted marquee of a New York jazz club."*

108. *The Mellow Pad*

1945–51. Oil on canvas, 26 x 42″
The Brooklyn Museum, New York.
Edith and Milton Lowenthal Collection

Davis used the composition of House and Street *(plate 8) as the armature to develop this painting. In his journal, on July 26, 1947, he wrote of his reasons: "*The Mellow Pad *was started on the premise that* House and Street *was a good painting and that its simplicity could be used as a base on which to develop new material. Out of this activity the theory of the Neutral Subject developed, and the entire role of Subject in relation to painting has been clarified." Hence, like its source,* The Mellow Pad *is divided into two parts, with such original naturalist elements as the brick storefront at the lower left now used as a design element.*

support him over the summer, since two museum sales had recently been delayed. "This leaves me penniless," he continues, "and I have no relatives or friends who are in a position to give direct assistance. The only asset I have is my work and if I can't get some reasonable breaks with that, the game is up." Although he made some money on a rug design, his "other efforts to get work of a kind I could do, decoration, writing, etc., [were] without success." He voices disappointment that he was not able to get sponsorship for his abstract-painting book nor for a project to print a set of color lithographs. "Thus the only function I have in the community, to paint and to educate in art, remains without support sufficient to sustain continued life." Moreover, he owes his landlord six months' rent: "It is only due to the unusual indulgence of my landlord that I am still indoors." He does not want charity, but "support for the

HOT AND COOL ABSTRACTION

108. *The Mellow Pad*

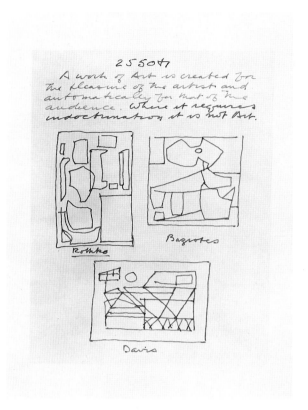

109. *Sketch of* Max *and of Rothko and Baziotes Paintings*

1950. Ink on paper, 11 x 8½"
Stuart Davis Papers, Index, 5 Feb 50. Fogg Art
Museum, Harvard University, Cambridge,
Massachusetts. Gift of Mrs. Stuart Davis

worthwhileness of my work," and he is convinced that his own art was meritorious—better in fact than other artists'—even if not always understood by the public.[6] His appeal underscores the fact that when the government curtailed its involvement with the arts and was closing down the Federal Art Project, the economy was not yet strong enough to encourage purchases by private patrons. Artists such as Davis, who depended upon their art for a living, suffered as a result.

Mrs. Sharkey showed the letter to Olin Dows, the federal administrator with whom Davis had sparred over artists' issues and who confessed to liking neither Davis nor his art. Yet when Dows heard of Davis's plight, he felt compelled to write to Solomon Guggenheim describing the "absolutely desperate" straits of the artist.[7] Nothing seems to have come of the appeal to Guggenheim. Davis might well have stayed clear of that particular patron, chary of repeating the experience he had with Baroness Rebay in 1934.

However, a sale came from an unexpected place. About 1940 the wife of the painter Niles Spencer, knowing of Davis's predicament, introduced him to John Hammond, a wealthy white jazz critic and recording entrepreneur who promoted African-American musicians such as Billie Holiday and Count Basie.[8] Hammond not only bought a painting from Davis but proceeded to lecture him on the subject of jazz. He was a tastemaker, the "Pope of Jazz," as Davis later called him, and the artist did not think it prudent to disagree. Hammond invited him to his place on Bleecker Street and played Bessie Smith records unfamiliar to Davis. He also introduced him to other jazz musicians, and Davis

HOT AND COOL ABSTRACTION

110. *Max No. 2*

1949. Oil on canvas, 12 x 16"
Washington University Art Gallery, St. Louis.
University purchase, Bixby Fund, 1952

got caught up in their nightlife. Through Niles Spencer's sister, Davis also heard the famous W. C. Handy play the piano; and through Walter Quirt, fellow artist and jazz enthusiast, he met Mildred Bailey.[9] His datebooks during these years note the jazz performances he attended: Louis Armstrong, Art Tatum, Earl Hines at the Savoy, and many jam sessions at the Vanguard, Nick's, and the Manhattan Center.

Davis's musical tastes encompassed a range of favorites. He also went to hear Bach's *B Minor Mass* at Carnegie Hall, which he noted was "perfect, a great abstract opera," and went to concerts of the avant-garde composer Edgard Varèse.[10] But it was jazz, specifically, that more and more he credited for influencing his own search for a style that was modern, alive, and American. He wrote to Hammond on March 12, 1940: "Earl Hines' piano playing has served me as a proof that art can exist, since 1928, when I heard his playing in a Louis Armstrong record, 'Save it pretty mama.'. . . Earl Hines represented to me the achievement of an abstract art of real order. His ability to take an anecdotal or sentimental song and turn it into a series of musical intervals of enormous variety has played an important part in helping me to formulate my own aspirations in painting." Davis wanted to make clear his appreciation of the roots of jazz in the African-American community, for he went on to say, "The art of the negroes through their music in America, and their African sculpture influence in modern art has been a major source of inspiration to me as a painter."[11]

Other artists recognized Davis's innovative use of jazz as an inspiration for working out formal, structural problems in painting. The African-American artist Romare Bearden recalled visiting Davis about 1940; the two men talked about the analogies between the structure and improvisations of jazz and those of painting. According to Albert Murray, Bearden credited Davis's encouragement for helping him to develop a "style of working with the separations between colors and the different values of a given color by studying the expressive use of interval in the piano style of Earl Hines."[12] Davis's journals in the 1940s are larded with references to the creativity of the jazz greats. On January 18, 1942, he noted the differences between illustration and art and saw the differences as analogous:

The public loves Tommy Dorsey and Sammy Kay but not Louis Armstrong or Earl Hines. Why is this? Dorsey makes them want to dance and exhibit themselves. S. Kay entertains them with games. Neither of these activities has anything to do with appreciation of music as a dimensional experience with sound. Loui [sic] and Earl play dance music, but in doing it they create, they invent new arabesques of tonal intervals as they go along. The public is not moved by this except as it refers to their dance. L & E do it for the experience of invention itself.[13]

In the fall of 1940, Davis began teaching at the New School for Social Research; it was a job he would continue until 1950. Although he never received the kind of acclaim for his teaching as had his mentors, Robert Henri and John Sloan, he developed a loyal following of students. Babette Eddleston, who took Davis's course, entitled "Modern Color-Space Composition in Drawing and Painting," in 1949, recalled both his cryptic "hmmms" in the classroom and also his dedication to art. When she entered class the first day she observed the teaching assistant preparing the still life: "He was placing every conceivable kind of object that can be found in an Art School prop room on a three by five foot table: Jugs, bottles, boxes, fake flowers, plaster casts, drapes, cord, strings, ribbons, etc. He placed things helter-skelter, one on top of another, until it was a holy mess with valleys and hills sometimes two or three feet high." From that still life, Davis expected the students to select and eliminate in order to learn to communicate what seemed interesting. To Eddleston it became a lesson in "focusing oneself completely when looking." One day, on the way to class, Eddleston found herself in the elevator with Davis and his friend George Wettling, the jazz drummer and painter. More loquacious than he was in the classroom, Davis began to expound on the pleasures of jazz and recommended nightspots for her to attend.[14] Art historian Naomi Miller recalls her experiences as a young art student at the New School. Davis's critiques consisted of such comments as "Why not a bit of lemon yellow in this spot?," and he was known on occasion to relocate his class to the corner church to listen to organ music by Bach.[15]

But Davis also gave sustained lectures (drafts of which were included with the journals) on his art theories and philosophy at the New School. For example, the draft of one New School talk, dated January 7, 1942, declares his intention to speak about the philosophical underpinnings, as well as the

In his Journal on September 4, 1951, Davis wrote: "Society is the amazing continuity between the Subjective Individual and the Display Window of History." A year later, Alfred H. Barr, Jr., who was curious about Davis's use of words in his paintings, asked the artist to comment. Writing on November 3, 1952, Davis described "champion" as having derived from a matchbook cover, and then offered explanations for the other words: "And the use of the word 'else' in this case was in harmony with my thought at the time that all subject matter is equal. The word 'else' was not selected but was given, since it did not obtrude by specific meanings ulterior to the general character of the picture, I used it. One could say that any four-letter word that filled that area would be as good . . . , but this would not be the case because . . . their specific meaning would have an importance that would divert the attention. . . . The word 'else,' while having different associations to different people, nevertheless has a fundamental dynamic content which consists of the thought that something else being possible there is an immediate sense of motion as an integrant of that thought."

HOT AND COOL ABSTRACTION

111. *Visa*

contemporary art-world context, of his artistic judgments: "Any theoretical formulations about the meaning of Art involve judgements about what is good and bad. We are forced to make a moral distinction between works of art—as their meaning refers to society as a whole. Otherwise our judgements are purely a matter of personal taste and there is really nothing to talk about. Pictures are not valued by the intrinsic worth of the materials of which they are made. They are valued for their Expressive Content—the Message they communicate." To Davis, all art had to satisfy a social need, and hence its value as "good or bad Art" depended on the expression of those social needs:

The basic social need is Survival and opposed to Dissolution—the struggle to keep alive on the planet. This struggle is carried on in many different ways, which take the form of political, industrial, and cultural action. These actions, in total, create a general cultural level—a civilization, which represents the essential needs of man in successful domination of his environment. In all great civilizations, art is present as fulfillment of a basic human need, and as an essential form of social communication. The painted Art Image communicates a certain kind of information which is not duplicated by any other form of communication. Its Content is unique.[16]

These thoughts are but a continuation of the analyses, begun in the 1930s, of the relationship of art to society.

The entry of the United States into World War II intensified his reflections about existing political systems. But without such forums as the American Artists Congress, he now seemed to carry on his battles within the pages of his journals. No doubt his students got an earful, since many of his thoughts find their way into his lecture notes.

By now, he had completely rejected communism, along with capitalism and fascism. To Davis: "They are unmoral because they place the organization of the material forces of modern science as an abstract good in itself, without relation to the human good which can be the only reason for their organization. The only cure for this condition will be the result of a spontaneous revolution of the human spirit, which will unseat existing political systems and re[e]stablish man, the individual man, as the subject matter of government and political action." To Davis the artist still has a role to play by creating an "awareness of humanism which will result in revolution directed toward real human progress."[17] Many artists and writers who had dropped away from radical politics in the early 1940s shared Davis's opinions—not just his blanket indictment of political systems but also the utopian vagueness of his vision of a future good society.

As John Lane has pointed out, Davis's New School appointment brought him in contact with Gestalt theory from the field of psychology.[18] He began to see "the *whole* picture" as a "psychological Gestalt which subsumes" the following elements: "topographical variation," "planar variety," "color intervals," "local color," "shapes and solids," "fields—light and shade: texture," and "words."[19] Gestalt theory gave Davis a new vocabulary with which to work out his space-color ideas, and it also severed his ties once and for all with Marxism. In response to the Marxist critique of Gestalt psychology developed by Stanley Diamond, who viewed Gestalt theories as static and unable to incorporate changing social reality, Davis countered with his own criticism that Diamond's brand of Marxism, because of its exclusive focus on social relations, "stifles individual creation and reaction."[20]

In 1941, Davis made his peace with Edith Halpert and went back to her Downtown Gallery. That year his friend Ralston Crawford, who was teaching at the Cincinnati Modern Art Society, recommended that Davis and Marsden Hartley be given retrospective exhibitions. From Cincinnati, the show traveled to Indiana University. It was the first major exhibition of Davis's work in seven years, and Halpert helped with transporting the paintings.

In his paintings of the early 1940s, Davis shifted the direction he had begun with *Swing Landscape* (plate 101). The paintings are still filled with shapes that float across the surface pulsating with color. But increasingly the forms and general layout of many of the 1940s compositions refer back to landscapes of the 1920s. Davis reorchestrated the compositions and added brighter colors. For example, the structure of *Report from Rockport* of 1940 (plate 103) was based on *Town Square* (plate 104), a watercolor from 1925–26, that had depicted the center of Rockport, a small town just beyond Gloucester on Cape Ann. The receding line of the buildings on either side, the pole in the front to the left of center, the tree in the middle distance, the gas pump at the right and the garage in the background are still visible in *Report from Rockport*. But instead of the somewhat static stage set, Davis has enlivened the scene with a variety of decorative squiggles, circles, stars, crosses, and arrows. He has, as they say, riffed on the earlier composition, just as his jazz musician friends could begin with the melody of a popular song, such as "Body and Soul," and then take off into flights of musical improvisation. Like jazz artists, Davis improvised within a structure. We might think of Rockport's "report" as being the sudden noise of rhythmic drum sounds, syncopated piano chatter, and blasting horns.

Hot Still-Scape for Six Colors—Seventh Avenue Style (plate 10), also painted in 1940, is another small work in the new jumping style that he was devising. The December 1940 issue of *Parnassus* reproduced the painting and included comments by Davis. The structural basis of the composition is *Egg Beater No. 2* (plate 67), with its diamond shape extending from the upper left to the lower right. Davis labored to get the colors in balance—often overpainting earlier tones until he got the effect he wanted.

When Halpert opened her gallery for the season with a group exhibition in September 1942, Davis was included along with fifteen other painters and two sculptors. Edward Alden Jewell, critic for the *New York Times,* praised Davis's *Arboretum by Flashbulb* of 1942 (plate 106), saying that the artist "outdoes himself as an abstractionist" and musing that perhaps Baroness Rebay would like the work. Davis, ever contentious and no doubt disliking the reference to Rebay, fired back a salvo to the editor that was printed in the *Times* on Septem-

112. *Rapt at Rappaport's*

1952. Oil on canvas, 52 x 40″
Hirshhorn Museum and Sculpture Garden,
Smithsonian Institution, Washington, D.C.
Gift of Joseph H. Hirshhorn Foundation, 1966

113. *Stele*

1956. Oil on canvas, 52 x 40″
Milwaukee Art Museum.
Gift of Harry Lynde Bradley

ber 27, 1942: "I have been repudiating the term 'abstraction,' as applied to my work, for fifteen years. . . . My pictures are partly the product of a number of abstract notions about the general character of color-space dimensionality, but I do not paint them to explain or describe these concepts. . . . Every direction, color position, size and shape in my pictures—all the serial configurations—are designed in accord with something I have seen, and wanted to recapture in terms of art, in the world in which we live."[21] As a postscript to Davis's letter, the editor urged the public to look at the picture and make its own decision.

Like *Ursine Park* of 1942 (location unknown), *Ultramarine* of 1943 (Pennsylvania Academy of the Fine Arts), and others in the series of horizontal paintings with densely packed shapes, Davis's *Arboretum* is a small work that seems large. The artist may have had in mind enlarging such pictures to mural size; earlier he had probed Mrs. Force of the Whitney to ascertain her interest in his murals. The painting jumps with abbreviated and hinted forms of trees, pathways, ponds, trellises, rocks, birds, distant buildings, and the indeterminate forms of the spaces between objects. Rudi Blesh, in his book on Davis of 1960, calls such pictures a "brilliantly kaleidoscopic synthesis of visual fragments."[22] While the painting is based on Davis's 1921 composition *Sword Plant* (collection Earl Davis),[23] the actual subject, according to the thrust of Davis's developing theories, is the act of experiencing anew that 1921 composition. In other words, the subject is the stimulating process of appropriation itself.

As Rudi Blesh also pointed out, "Just at the time that the jive-talk of musicians began circulating outside the jazz world, Davis began creating 'jive' titles" with alliterations, puzzle words, puns, and special jazz terms.[24] Davis had previously incorporated words of popular jazz songs, such as Duke Ellington's "It don't mean a thing, if it ain't got that swing," in his 1932 *American Painting* (plate 92), but in the 1940s the words float free from any connecting phrases and challenge the viewer to complete them.

In February 1943, Davis's first solo exhibition of recent work in nine years opened at the Downtown Gallery on East Fifty-first Street. It was not just an opening, but a literal jam session with musicians playing throughout the day. Amateurs performed, such as Ellis Larkin and the cartoonist Bill Steig,[25] as well as, in Davis's words, "a number of Grade A jazz musicians . . . W. C. Handy, Mildred Bailey, Red Norvo, George Wettling, Duke Ellington and Pete Johnson, king of boogie-woogie pianists."[26] Among the art-world figures who showed up was Piet Mondrian, then living in New York as an expatriate from wartime Europe and an enthusiast of American jazz, particularly boogie-woogie. Davis considered it "a great honor to have the presence of an internationally famous European artist,"[27] even if he did not agree with Mondrian's ideas, the subject of several private journal entries.[28]

The critics got the point—almost. Emily Genauer of the *World-Telegram* wrote: "Davis hoped that guests would see how the irregular geometrical shapes and piebald colors of his compositions . . . echo the rhythms and tempo of swing music. And they do, too. There is the same two-dimensional quality, the same tangential patterning, the same quicksilver variations within a compact frame—and the same lack of anything in the least resembling emotional and intellectual depth." Carlyle Burrows of the *Herald Tribune* commented: "If you feel the nervous spirit, the hectic movement which jazz and swing celebrate in modern music, you doubtless have sensed what Davis intends his pictures to convey." Peyton Boswell, the conservative critic of the *Art Digest* granted that Davis's paintings were like jazz but objected to "having jazz confused with music—which, I suppose, is what conservatives say about modernism and art."[29] By saying that jazz was to traditional music as modernism was to traditional art, the critic had stumbled on the truth.

The most thoughtful criticism came from Robert M. Coates, writing for *The New Yorker*. He pointed out that of the twenty paintings in the Downtown exhibition, many were close to the forms of nature. But with such paintings as *Arboretum by Flashbulb*, "if you haven't got abstraction, you've got something so near as to be practically indistinguishable from it." He then went on to state that Davis "certainly belongs among the top ten American painters alive today." Clement Greenberg, soon to be the champion of the New York School, as the Abstract Expressionists were to be called, found words of praise for Davis. To Greenberg, Davis had for too long stayed within a Dufy-esque formula of "line against flat areas of high, dry, acid color." The critic liked particularly *Arboretum by Flashbulb* and *Report from Rockport*.[30]

The Museum of Modern Art took notice of Davis at the same time the museum was creating its canon for modern art. In 1943, Alfred H. Barr, Jr., wrote his influential booklet *What Is Modern Painting?* and included a reproduction of Davis's *Summer Landscape* of 1930 (plate 73), which the museum had purchased in 1940, along with a photograph of the site in Gloucester (plate 74). In his text, Barr compared Davis's work with a conventional landscape and concluded that "it is not hard to decide which shows the more imagination, the greater will to select, control, arrange and organize"—all the hallmarks, to Barr, of modernism.[31]

The Museum of Modern Art helped Davis's career in other ways as well. In 1942, the Modern had commissioned a rug design, *Flying Carpet*, for an exhibition of modernist rugs. Barr would also know of Davis's solid reputation in the art world and of his inclusion in the exhibition "Masters of Abstract Art," held at the Helena Rubinstein Art Center in New York. It was probably about this time that James Johnson Sweeney began to plan a retrospective of Davis's work for the Modern for the fall of 1945.

In the meantime, with the country preoccupied with winning World War II, museum curators organized large exhibitions as part of the effort to boost civilian morale. The Metropolitan Museum was host to the huge "Artists for Victory" show of some fourteen hundred artists held in December 1942 that included Davis's *Bass Rocks No. 1* of 1939 (Wichita Art Museum). In 1944 the "Portrait of America" exhibition was staged, under the sponsorship of Pepsi-Cola; Davis won first prize for his 1937 painting *The Terminal* (plate 97).

James Johnson Sweeney included fifty-two paintings, plus the Modern's rug, in the Davis retrospective held at the Museum of Modern Art during Octo-

114. *American Painting*

1932–51. Oil on canvas, 40 x 50¼″
Joslyn Art Museum, Omaha.
University of Nebraska at Omaha Collection

*See plate 92 for a reproduction of the
painting as originally done in 1932.*

ber and November 1945. Sweeney's catalogue essay, the longest article on Davis to date, interwove biographical material with an analysis of his artwork within the context of developing European modernism. Generous quotations from Davis's own autobiography, which the artist was then writing for the American Artists Group monograph series, guided Sweeney's narration.

Reviews of the retrospective came from old friends. Holger Cahill wrote a long article for *Art News* calling Davis's exhibition "more than a long backward glance at the work of a leading contemporary artist." To Cahill it was "the biography of an era, one of the most vital and revolutionary in the history of American art. . . . [The exhibition] is vigorous, exciting as a jam session, filled with keen observation and humor."[32]

From the left came a review in *New Masses* written by Ad Reinhardt, who called Davis "one of our 'first' American moderns." Reinhardt, himself an abstract painter, liked the fact that Davis's paintings demanded "more participation, more awareness on the part of the onlooker." However, he ends the review on a sober note: "Our contemporary 'art world' forces painters to exploit their individuality and peculiarity, and unfortunately one is always 'on one's own.' Davis has always known the value of group activity, though, and was once conspicuous in the organized combating of Fascism, bigotry, narrow political and aesthetic ideas. His present political inactivity and his lack of relation to the artists' group is regrettable for a painter of his integrity and stature."[33] Davis was obviously missed by some of his old comrades.

Davis's Museum of Modern Art exhibition was followed by a smaller retrospective at the Downtown Gallery, which opened January 29, 1946, and consisted of drawings, watercolors, and gouaches, including studies for his Egg Beater series. Together, these two exhibitions reminded the public of Davis's considerable achievement.

Davis's life at this time seemed to have settled into a pattern. He painted in his studio at 43 Seventh Avenue while his wife, Roselle, worked as a librarian and social worker. Errands, his teaching job at the New School, and visits to galleries took him out of the house. In the evenings he went out drinking with his buddies or with Roselle and listened to jazz.

His financial situation, moreover, was becoming secure. Edith Halpert took care of sending his paintings out to loan exhibitions and was ever alert to opportunities for him. Halpert encouraged new patrons, such as Edith and Milton Lowenthal, who came to her gallery after they had seen Davis's *Bass Rocks No. 1* at the "Artists for Victory" exhibition. The Lowenthals were given first choice of Davis's work and bought *Report from Rockport* (plate 103), *Arboretum by Flashbulb* (plate 106), and *The Mellow Pad* (plate 108).[34] During the 1950s, William H. Lane, a friend of Halpert's, purchased a number of works including *Egg Beater No. 3* (plate 65). In January 1946, Davis made for the Whitney Museum a list of the public and private collections that held his work. The universities, museums, and public institutions numbered at least twenty-one, with several works owned by the Whitney, the Modern, and the Phillips Collection. Private collectors included not only the usual wealthy patrons—Mrs. John D.

115. *Tropes de Teens*

1956. Oil on canvas, 45¼ x 60¼"
Hirshhorn Museum and Sculpture Garden,
Smithsonian Institution, Washington, D.C.
Gift of Joseph H. Hirshhorn Foundation, 1966

Rockefeller, Jr., Walter P. Chrysler, Jr., and Roy Neuberger—but also a surprising variety of others: old acquaintances Henry McBride, Holger Cahill, and Elliot Paul, artists Louis Guglielmi and William Steig, as well as jazz man John Hammond.[35]

More and more the established, mainline art world bestowed upon him awards and honors. To many critics, aware of the surge of abstract paintings in postwar America, Davis's works were appealing because they still had recognizable forms. In 1947, *Life* focused on Davis in an article entitled "Why Artists Are Going Abstract: The Case of Stuart Davis." The author, Winthrop Sargeant, explained that art began to "go abstract" in the nineteenth century in reaction to the realism of photography; the camera freed painters to leave documentary behind and become more inventive. The case of Davis should be easy, Sargeant reassures his readership, since he "goes about painting a picture in very much the spirit grandma had when she was making a patchwork quilt, placing squares and oblongs of color where they will contribute tastefully to the over-all pattern." Sargeant granted that Davis was "somewhat more skillful and imagi-

116. *Allée*

1955. Oil on canvas, 8 x 30'
Drake University, Des Moines

The mural was originally installed in the university's North Dining Room.

native than grandma. He knows how to produce striking contrasts and how to lead the eye through interesting little adventures in observation."[36] Davis's specific response to Sargeant's essay is not known, but he no doubt would have reasserted his space-color theories and stressed that observation of the world around him—signs, gasoline pumps, airplanes—was a crucial ingredient in his paintings. In 1948, *Look* magazine announced the results of a poll of museum directors and art critics to determine the "Ten Best Artists." Davis placed number four, after John Marin, Max Weber, and Yasuo Kuniyoshi, and was followed on the list by Ben Shahn, Charles Burchfield, George Grosz, and Franklin Watkins, with Lionel Feininger and Jack Levine tied for tenth. The winning artists were also secretly polled, and Davis placed seventh on that list.

Since Davis had disavowed radical politics in early 1940, when he resigned from the American Artists Congress, he was not the target of the congressional investigations into domestic communism during the late 1940s and the 1950s. Yet his name was included among the list of subversives read into the *Congressional Record* on May 13, 1947, since he had been a member of the advisory board of the John Reed Club School and had submitted drawings to *The Masses, The Liberator,* and *New Masses.*[37]

With the advantage of hindsight, we can see the later 1940s as a transitional era for Davis. While he and others of his generation were receiving kudos from the popular press, the critics were turning to younger abstract painters. Clement Greenberg, who had offered moderate praise for Davis's 1943 Downtown Gallery show, wrote less than enthusiastically about Davis's Museum of Modern Art retrospective in 1945. Greenberg saw Davis's work as decorative and equated him with Alexander Calder. At this time Greenberg was beginning to champion the younger, "heroic" artists, such as Jackson Pollock and Willem de Kooning, who did "ambitious," avant-garde painting. By 1955, Greenberg praised the younger men because they had all moved away from "that canon of rectilinear and curvilinear regularity in drawing and design which Cubism had imposed on almost all previous abstract art."[38] Davis, by this criterion, was becoming a historical artifact. When John Baur wrote his *Revolution and Tradition in Modern American Art* in 1951, he declared that "Davis's art summarizes the best qualities of American abstraction in the 1920s," but while Davis and Feininger "have established well-deserved reputations in their field, their direct influence on younger painters has been relatively small."[39]

Davis saw what was happening in the New York galleries, and he was curious about the younger Abstract Expressionists. He went to exhibitions of the younger men, and he made sketches of William Baziotes's and Mark Rothko's paintings (see plate 109). He had, after all, been good friends with Gorky, and Franz Kline was a neighbor. He also went to the Cedar Bar, a popular hangout of the Abstract Expressionists. But the style was not for him. In his interview with Harlan Phillips, he maintained that "abstract expressionism . . . didn't bother me. I just preferred the cubist structural approach to things and their more familiar daily references to known objects." Picasso was still his guide: "There's always something in his pictures that indicates this world, not some other, not the insane asylum, or Sigmund Freud. . . . It's always a world we know about. My nature leads me to adhere to that kind of an attitude." Davis added that Philip Guston and Willem de Kooning had "a lot of ability," but he did not regard Abstract Expressionism "as the pathway to some great discovery."[40]

But while the style of Abstract Expressionism might not have appealed to him, his theoretical writings in the late 1940s and early 1950s would become more introverted. He became less concerned with questions of the relationship of art to social organization, and more obsessed with what he called the "C complex of intuitive color-space ratio balances."[41] Over and over he advanced the proposition that subject matter could achieve a condition of neutrality. His ruminations were not far from the theories developing around Abstract Expressionism when he stated: "Whatever the emotional content of the experience originally derived from Subject, it is changed into the content of emotions associated with the experience of realizing the balances in the act of painting itself."[42] Both Davis and the Abstract Expressionists sought to express "the act of painting itself"—a phrase commonly heard in the rhetoric of critics in the postwar and Cold War period. But Davis differed from the Abstract Expressionists in his Apollonian discipline and dialectical application of theory to practice, rather than, as he would see it, the Dionysian excesses of that younger group of abstract artists.

117. *The Paris Bit*

1959. Oil on canvas, 40 x 60″
Whitney Museum of American Art, New York.
Purchase, with funds from the Friends of the
Whitney Museum of American Art, 59.38

Famous Artists Magazine, *published by
the Famous Artists School (a correspondence school operating out of Westport,
Connecticut), asked Davis to name his
favorite work. He chose* The Paris Bit:
*"Any painting I am working on is my
favorite. An artist sees his purpose, and
the meaning of it, as a continuity of
experience. It is the ability to make new
pictures, in which experience [in] making the previous ones is brought to life
and developed in the present, that gives
him the greatest pleasure."*

Also, unlike the Abstract Expressionists, Davis was not a snob about commercial ventures, since they brought in revenue. In 1946, the Container Corporation of America had commissioned him to do the Pennsylvania design for
their series of promotional ads focused on the individual American states and
territories. The series—advertisements made classy by the involvement of leading artists—was published in such magazines as *Fortune* and *Time*. He also lent
his name and image to Grumbacher, the maker of artists' supplies, which published his picture and testimonial in Grumbacher advertisements. And in 1954,
Davis joined the faculty of the Famous Artists School in Westport, an art correspondence school that advertised itself on matchbook covers and with which he
would be associated until 1964.

The Davises, who had always lived modestly on the top floor of 43 Seventh
Avenue, had a son in 1952, whom they named George Earl, after Davis's friends
the jazz pianist Earl Hines and the drummer George Wettling. The baby was a

novelty for Davis, and he seems to have doted on his young son. The family obviously needed more space, and in 1955, when Davis received the commission to paint a mural for Drake University, the family moved to a studio in an apartment house that had been built for artists on Sixty-seventh Street, off Central Park West. Here Davis had a working space with a two-story ceiling in which to paint the Drake mural, *Allée* (plate 116), and in 1957, the *Combination Concrete* mural (plate 122) for the H. J. Heinz Research Center in Pittsburgh.

The Drake mural was commissioned by Eero Saarinen, the architect then designing the Drake University campus in Des Moines, Iowa. Davis traveled to Des Moines to view the proposed site and was impressed by "the whiteness of the room—its ceiling and walls—the black floors, the blue sky outside those high windows, and the red rectangles of the brick dormitories." The physical setting influenced his choice of colors—blue, white, red, and black—and the rectilinear and uncluttered composition. He provided a statement for the university that was published in a pamphlet:

Allée is a French word meaning an alley or long vista. It is a long painting. Its length over-powered my studio and made a deep impression on my mind. Also, there is another French word with the same sound which means "go." I like this association. I like the variety, the animation, the vigorous spirit which is part of college life. This feeling of energy and vigor was in my mind during the painting of the mural. . . . Do not look for meanings and symbolism which are not there. Instead, look for the color-space relationships which give the painting its vigorous tone and its structural feeling. The placing of the figures and colors were done with feelings and thoughts which were the product of my interest in life. The meaning of the mural will change as the viewer gives meaning to it.

As Davis worked in his New York studio, he thought of his intended audience at the campus, the "intellectual issues debated with vigor, of football, poetry, jazz music, of excitement." Viewing the work after it was installed, he was pleased with the results.[43]

Although the critical kingmakers were busy anointing other artists, Davis in the decade of the 1950s garnered even more awards, prizes, and prestigious commissions than in the 1940s. In 1951, he taught at the art school at Yale, and his work was included in the first Bienal de São Paulo. In 1952, he won a John Simon Guggenheim Memorial Foundation fellowship and also had a solo exhibition at the American Pavilion at the 1952 Venice Biennale. In 1956, he was elected to the National Institute of Arts and Letters and was included in that year's Venice Biennale. In 1957 he had a retrospective exhibition at the Walker Art Center in Minneapolis; in 1958 and again in 1960, he won the Solomon R. Guggenheim Museum International Award.

In his studio at West Sixty-seventh Street, Davis received many friends, curators, and critics who came by to interview him. In 1953, *Art News* had sent a writer and photographer to focus on him for the magazine's "Paints a Picture" series. The lead photograph pictures Davis in a corner of his studio, green eye-shade pulled down over his forehead as he mixes his paints while watching television (see plate 11). The *Art News* writer, Dorothy Gees Seckler, explained that for the painting *Rapt at Rappaport's* (plate 112) Davis used a sketch he had made at Gloucester thirty years before (*Still Life with Saw*, 1922; collection Earl Davis). He told her that "'remembered shapes and colors, having nothing to do with the original point of departure, influenced what I put down, and even associations from sounds and imagined movements contributed a part in the day-to-day changes on the canvas.'" First Davis made black outlines on the white canvas, then he began to paint in the green which he explained: "'There might have been a dozen reasons why green took precedence in my mind at that time. . . . It could have been somebody else's picture, a mood of depression or elation, or a green traffic light.'"[44] Further, Davis explained that he painted in the word "any" because he wanted letters or a word but he did not want to use one with too many associations. The words he used to describe his painting process include "actions" and "intervals." When he had finished the work he sent it off to the Whitney's 1952 Annual exhibition, and then began another, *Semé* of 1953 (The Metropolitan Museum of Art, New York), with the same motifs, explaining that "'it's the same thing as when a musician takes a sequence of notes and makes many variations on them.'"

Except for commissioned paintings during the 1950s, Davis frequently began with a composition from an earlier work. For example, *Owh! in San Pao* of 1951 (plate 12) was based on *Percolator* of 1927 (plate 62). Whereas the earlier versions set up compositions with textured planes (dots, dashes, and suggestions of shading) that symbolized the spaces of sky, clouds, water, and so on,

119. Study for *Package Deal*

1956. Ink on paper, 6 x 4"
Collection Earl Davis, courtesy
Salander-O'Reilly Galleries, New York

In 1956, Fortune *magazine commissioned Davis and six other artists to make original artworks based on commercial packaging. According to the interview conducted by James Elliott with Davis, the artist brought home a bag of groceries, arranged them in his studio, and began to draw the shapes of the products, the logos, and letters of the packaging. He did over two dozen drawings—arranging and rearranging the shapes of the containers and the placement of the words on them so that the words became independent shapes freed from both containers and context.*

HOT AND COOL ABSTRACTION

120. *Premiere*

1957. Oil on canvas, 58 x 50"
Los Angeles County Museum of Art. Museum
Purchase, Art Museum Council Fund

*From his drawings of packaged goods,
Davis painted the gouache called* Package Goods *of 1956 (private collection).
He later enlarged that image to make*
Premiere.

the 1950s versions are flatly painted with large crosses, circles, and letters.[45] In
the late 1950s and in the 1960s, until his death in 1964, Davis made a number
of large paintings with a limited palette and which use words, letters, and num-
bers. But before his death he also won a competition for his smallest design—
for a five-cent U.S. postage stamp honoring the fine arts.[46]

Whether he was aware of it or not, Davis's life extended beyond the glory
years of Abstract Expressionism, and critics far younger than Clement Greenberg took notice of him. Gene Goosen, a critic close to a younger generation
of artists challenging the Abstract Expressionists, wrote a monograph on Davis
in 1959 in which he stated that "at a moment when vagueness about pictorial
structure is being used to support all kinds of rationalizations after the fact,
Davis' clean-cut assertions make weaker painters uneasy. The best of the
younger artists, however, recognize and respect what he stands for."[47] And in
1962, Donald Judd, then a young artist developing a precise geometric art,

121. Stuart Davis in the studio with *Combination Concrete* on the easel. c. 1958

122. *Combination Concrete*

1958. Oil on canvas, 71 x 53"
Private collection

The compositional armature and some of the iconography for Combination Concrete *are from Davis's* Landscape *of 1922 (plate 46). In the 1958 painting all the basic shapes of the earlier version are there, including the zigzag at the upper-right center, the grid of dots in the lower center, and the signs saying* GO SLOW *and* CURVE. *Davis exclaims to the viewer (note the exclamation point) that what is "new" is the "drawing" in paint that interacts with that original armature.*

praised a Davis exhibition for the lessons it could teach younger artists.[48]

The critic who perhaps got closest to Davis in his last years was Brian O'Doherty, who wrote for the *New York Times*. O'Doherty met Davis, who impressed him as a "jowly, roly-poly, shy bulldog, tough, gravelly-voiced, etc." O'Doherty knew that Davis was ill, and he visited him in his studio as well as in the hospital when Davis had an operation on a leg ulcer.[49] O'Doherty was in his office at the *Times* when the obituary writer called one day to ask whether or not Davis was a "famous artist"—famous enough to get a front-page notice. Davis had died the day before, on June 24, 1964, of a stroke. O'Doherty was stunned, and next to the official obituary published on the inside pages of the

HOT AND COOL ABSTRACTION

Times, O'Doherty wrote his own tribute: "His death removes one of the limited company of major painters America has produced. . . . He was never out of date. Whatever happened in the world of art already seemed to have a precedent in his painting." O'Doherty was touched by the contrast between Davis's tough-guy personality and nuanced intellect: "The deceptively matter-of-fact exterior (he looked like someone who was going to go and shoot craps any minute) concealed a classic spirit, a spirit of the sort that could find some principle of eternal order in the neon wilderness of Times Square. He searched disorder for its unifying principle."[50] The "unifying principle" that Davis found was "the amazing continuity," a phrase he used in his journals and in his painting *Visa* (plate 111). The interconnectedness of art and life, of the past and the present, of words and images was, to Davis, just that—amazing.

123. Stuart and Earl Davis in the studio with *Fin* on the easel. 1964

Davis's career spanned six decades of American modernism. Encouraged by artist parents and by Henri and Sloan, the young Davis prowled the city streets for pictorial ideas. He argued art and politics in the radical, bohemian atmosphere of Greenwich Village, and he listened to African-American ragtime and jazz. When the Armory Show pointed him in the direction of modernism, it gave him "the same kind of excitement," he later said, that he had experienced when listening to the "numerical precisions" of African-American piano players. He then took up Cubism's structural premise and, working with American subjects from everyday life, experimented for the next three decades to develop his signature style. These years sharpened his belief in the international character of art; in the 1930s, his involvement with radical artists' organizations fueled his conviction that art belongs to all the people. During the 1940s, his art came to full maturity, and he learned to incorporate, in visual terms, the rhythmic beats, melodic flourishes, and improvisational techniques of jazz. And the argot of jazz musicians, both black and white, became for Davis the language most suitable for expressing his ideas about art. By now he had thoroughly internalized the most dynamic aspects of popular culture, and was structuring this experience into a lively, democratic, and urban art.

Toward the end of his life, there was no falling off of his artistic abilities or imaginative stratagems, although poor health at times slowed his production. History will no doubt concur with the judgment of the artist Will Barnet, who knew him during the middle decades of the century: "Of the modern painters, he was one of the few who got better, more inventive and powerful, like Titian, and able to sustain the energy in his work. . . . Stuart Davis gave himself totally. Not just with intellectualism—but also with passion. You can feel it in his work."[51] More than thirty years after his death, the syntax of his painting—its colored shapes, receding and projecting planes, and nonassociational words— still communicates Davis's upbeat and altogether democratic faith in the ability of ordinary people to delight in an art of contemporary life.

Notes to the Text

In the notes the following abbreviations have been used: *AAA* for the Archives of American Art, Smithsonian Institution, Washington, D.C.; *WMAA* for the Archives of the Whitney Museum of American Art, New York; *MoMA* for the Archives of the Museum of Modern Art, New York; *Fogg Papers* for the Stuart Davis Papers, Fogg Art Museum, Harvard University Art Museums (Gift of Mrs. Stuart Davis; All rights reserved by the President and Fellows of Harvard University).

Introduction:
The Making of a Hip Modernist

1. Transcript of interviews between Stuart Davis and Harlan B. Phillips, May and June 1962, p. 15 (Stuart Davis Papers [Restricted], AAA), hereinafter cited as *Phillips transcript*. Extensive excerpts from this interview are published in "An Interview with Stuart Davis," *Archives of American Art Journal* 31, no. 2 (1991), pp. 4–13.
2. According to the archival records of East Orange High School, Davis attended that institution from September 1908 to April 1909. Since for many years he gave his birthdate as 1894, rather than the actual date of 1892, there has been confusion until now about his high-school attendance. I am grateful to Bernadette Cheek for sending me a copy of Davis's transcript of grades.
3. For an overview of the Greenwich Village art scene, see Arthur Frank Wertheim, *The New York Little Renaissance: Iconoclasm, Modernism, and Nationalism in American Culture, 1908–1917* (New York: New York University Press, 1976), and Steven Watson, *Strange Bedfellows: The First*

American Avant-Garde (New York: Abbeville, 1991).
4. "American Art," *The Soil* 1 (December 1916), p. 3. Such strings of "American" subjects may recall Ralph Waldo Emerson's essay "The Poet" (1842) and Walt Whitman's poems in *Leaves of Grass* (1855).
5. Phillips transcript, pp. 149–50.
6. "The Place of Abstract Painting in America" (letter to Henry McBride), *Creative Art* 6 (February 1930); in Diane Kelder, ed. *Stuart Davis: A Documentary Monograph* (New York: Praeger, 1971), p. 110.
7. Helen Farr Sloan, interview with the author, Wilmington, Delaware, September 21, 1993.
8. Phillips transcript, p. 13.
9. Lewis Kachur, "The Language of Stuart Davis: Writing/Drawing," in Karen Wilkin and Lewis Kachur, *The Drawings of Stuart Davis: The Amazing Continuity* (New York: The American Federation of Arts and Harry N. Abrams, Inc., 1992), p. 30. Information about the more than six hundred paintings that Davis made during his lifetime will appear in a forthcoming catalogue raisonné (date of publication to be announced). A selection of Davis's writings was republished in Kelder, *Stuart Davis*. The original writings have been microfilmed by the AAA and the Houghton Library, Harvard University. The artist's son, Earl Davis, also maintains an archive of Davis papers and memorabilia.
10. Stieglitz had shown modern art at his Little Galleries of the Photo Secession at 291 Fifth Avenue, but the general public was unaware of his exhibitions.
11. Davis, *Stuart Davis*, p. [12].

12. See Richard J. Powell, *The Blues Aesthetic: Black Culture and Modernism* (Washington, D.C.: Washington Project for the Arts, 1989).
13. See Phillips transcript, pp. 41–43. Regarding Williams and Walker in the history of minstrelsy and the black community, see Nathan Irvin Huggins, *Harlem Renaissance* (New York: Oxford University Press, 1971), pp. 280 ff; see also Eric Lott, *Love and Theft: Blackface Minstrelsy and the American Working Class* (New York: Oxford University Press, 1993).
14. Phillips transcript, pp. 41–43.
15. The spelling, punctuation, and capitalization are Davis's. Hence, "Mon" could refer to the abbreviation of that day of the week or could be a dialect spelling for "man." Transcripts of the calendar sheets were provided to me by Earl Davis.
16. For an analysis of these oral traditions, see Roger D. Abrahams, *Talking Black* (Rowley, Mass.: Newbury House, 1976). Abrahams gives an example of such "capping," or "playing the dozens," p. 20: "Oh man, don't mess with me, I'll jump down your throat, grate your tonsils, bust your stomach, and tickle your feet." Henry Louis Gates, Jr., has elaborated on this tradition in *The Signifying Monkey: A Theory of African-American Literary Criticism* (New York: Oxford University Press, 1988). See also Lott, *Love and Theft*. Rap is simply an extension of these traditions.
17. Davis, interview by John Wingate on the radio program "Nightbeat," 1957. I am grateful to Earl Davis for sending me a copy of this tape.
18. When queried by Wingate as

to whether he cared about the "man in the street," Davis answered that he didn't think about his public while making a work, "but the more the men in the street enjoy it after I do it, the happier I'll be about it" (ibid.).

I. The Apprentice Years: 1909–1920

1. Phillips transcript, p. 14.
2. For example, John Sloan noted in his diary that on New Year's Day, 1906, he and Dolly had dinner with the Davis family, including Stuart, who had just turned thirteen; see Bruce St. John, ed., *John Sloan's New York Scene: From the Diaries, Notes and Correspondence, 1906–1913* (New York: Harper & Row, 1965), p. 3.
3. See the Introduction, note 2.
4. See Elisabeth Milroy, *Painters of a New Century: The Eight and American Art* (Milwaukee: Milwaukee Art Museum, 1992).
5. Quoted in John R. Lane, *Stuart Davis: Art and Art Theory* (Brooklyn, N.Y.: The Brooklyn Museum, 1978), p. 9
6. Davis, *Stuart Davis*, p. [4]. Robert Hunter, "The Rewards and Disappointments of the Ashcan School: The Early Career of Stuart Davis," in Lowery Stokes Sims, *Stuart Davis, American Painter* (New York: The Metropolitan Museum of Art, 1991), p. 34, discusses Davis's fellow students in Henri's school.
7. See William Inness Homer, *Robert Henri and His Circle* (Ithaca, N.Y.: Cornell University Press, 1969), pp. 172, 187, 192; see also Lane, *Stuart Davis*, pp. 12–14.
8. See Marianne Doezema, *George Bellows and Urban America* (New Haven, Conn.: Yale University Press, 1992),

pp. 113–21. The catalogue of the 1918 Independents show, which included 499 paintings, drawings, and sculpture is reproduced in Delaware Art Center, *The Fiftieth Anniversary of the Exhibition of Independent Artists in 1910* (Wilmington, Del.: Delaware Art Center, 1960).

9. Davis, *Stuart Davis*, pp. [4, 6].

10. Milton W. Brown, *The Story of the Armory Show* (New York: Abbeville, 1988), p. 260, lists the five watercolors.

11. "The 'Modern' Spirit in Art," *Harper's Weekly*, March 15, 1913; in Barbara Rose, ed., *Readings in American Art: 1900–1975* (New York: Holt, Rinehart & Winston, 1975), p. 72.

12. "A Layman's Views of an Art Exhibition," *The Outlook*, March 29, 1913, p. 719.

13. Arthur Jerome Eddy, *Cubists and Post-Impressionism* (Chicago: A. C. McClurg & Co., 1914), p. 64.

14. Davis, *Stuart Davis*, p. [12].

15. See Marius de Zayas, *African Negro Art: Its Influence on Modern Art* (New York: Modern Gallery, 1916); and Marius de Zayas, "How, When, and Why Modern Art Came to New York," introduction and notes by Francis M. Naumann, *Arts Magazine* 54 (April 1980), pp. 109–12.

16. Rebecca Zurier, *Art for "The Masses": A Radical Magazine and Its Graphics, 1911–1917* (Philadelphia: Temple University Press, 1988), pp. 32-37.

17. The clipping, with illustration, is reproduced as fig. 3 in Richard J. Powell, *The Blues Aesthetic: Black Culture and Modernism* (Washington, D.C.: Washington Project for the Arts, 1989), p. 22.

18. Quoted above. A photograph of the Joplin sketch is at the Whitney Museum of American Art, New York.

19. See Max Eastman, *Enjoyment of Living* (New York: Harper & Brothers, 1948), p. 412.

20. Davis, *Stuart Davis*, pp. [14, 16].

21. Ibid., p. [16].

22. Phillips transcript, p. 77.

23. Ibid., p. 84.

24. Davis, *Stuart Davis*, p. [16]. In the Phillips transcript, p. 70, Davis said: "Demuth had

already been to Europe, and being the sophisticated esthetic type that he was—he moved in circles of the 'hip' people—about art, so that whatever conversations we had about this matter he was able to give me sympathetic and knowledgeable replies which were very important."

25. *New York Sun*, January 25, 1914; quoted in Davis, *Stuart Davis*, p. [8], where Davis states the year as 1913.

26. Charles Caffin, in the *New York American*, October 19, 1914; Stuart Davis Papers (Scrapbook), AAA. Also quoted in Davis, *Stuart Davis*, pp. [8, 10].

27. Zurier, *Art for "The Masses,"* p. 52. Young's statement gave rise to the name "Ashcan School" for Henri's circle.

28. Max Eastman, *Heroes I Have Known: Twelve Who Lived Great Lives* (New York: Simon & Schuster, 1942), p. 58.

29. Clipping from a Philadelphia newspaper, dated February 8, 1917; Stuart Davis Papers (Scrapbook), AAA.

30. Clipping from the *New York World*, April 23, 1918; Stuart Davis Papers (Scrapbook), AAA. See also Zurier, *Art for "The Masses,"* pp. 61–64.

31. Lewis Kachur, "America's Argenteuil: Artists at Gloucester," *Arts Magazine* 56 (March 1982), pp. 138–39.

32. Davis, *Stuart Davis*, p. [16].

33. For information about the Sloan crowd in Gloucester, see Britt Crews, "The Red Cottage," in *The Red Cottage* (Gloucester, Mass.: Cape Ann Historical Association, 1992), n.p.

34. See Crews, *The Red Cottage*, n.p. I am grateful to Britt Crews for sending me a photocopy of Maratta's 1913 brochure, from the archives of the Cape Ann Historical Association, Gloucester.

35. On a postcard to Glenn Coleman, dated June 21, 1917 (collection Earl Davis), Davis asks whether Coleman was "doing photography," and adds: "I have just started to print but have got nothing yet." A photograph of Davis holding his Twin Lens Reflex Camera, c. 1930 (collection Earl Davis), was shown at the Phillips Collection, Wash-

ington, D.C., in June and July 1994.

36. Quoted in James F. O'Gorman, "Parnassus on Ledge Road: The Life and Times of East Gloucester's Gallery-on-the-Moors, 1916–1922," in *The Red Cottage*, n.p. Coburn's article was from the *Boston Sunday Herald*, September 10, 1916.

37. See Judith K. Zilczer, "Modern Art and Its Sources: Exhibitions in New York, 1910–1925," appendix to William I. Homer, ed., *Avant-Garde Painting and Sculpture in America, 1910–25* (Wilmington, Del.: Delaware Art Museum, 1975).

38. See the catalogue *The Forum Exhibition of Modern American Painters* (New York: Anderson Galleries, 1916). Among the other artists included in the show were Ben Benn, Thomas H. Benton, Oscar Bluemner, Andrew Dasburg, Marsden Hartley, Alfred Maurer, Henry McFee, George F. Of, Morgan Russell, Charles Sheeler, Abraham Walkowitz, and William Zorach.

39. Quoted in Lane, *Stuart Davis*, p. 12; Fogg Papers, Index, 1918.

40. Davis illustrated the newspaper reports on the *Masses* ball and the Dell production; see *The World*, December 27, 1914, and February 28, 1915, respectively; Stuart Davis Papers (Scrapbook), AAA.

41. For information on the team of Mrs. Whitney and Mrs. Force, see Roberta K. Tarbell, "Gertrude Vanderbilt Whitney as Patron," in Patricia Hills and Roberta K. Tarbell, *The Figurative Tradition and the Whitney Museum of American Art* (New York: Whitney Museum of American Art, 1980), and Avis Berman, *Rebels on Eighth Street: Juliana Force and the Whitney Museum of American Art* (New York: Atheneum, 1990).

42. Stuart Davis, "Recollections of the Whitney" (transcript of WNYC radio interview with John I. H. Baur, 1953 [WMAA]), p. 4.

43. Ibid., p. 2; WMAA.

44. Clipping marked *New York Globe*, January 6, 1917; Stuart Davis Papers (Scrapbook), AAA. See fig. 99 in Sims, *Stu-*

art Davis, American Painter, p. 138. A photograph of another version is in WMAA.

45. "Critics Laud Young Artist," *Newark Morning Ledger*, June 1, 1918; Stuart Davis Papers (Scrapbook), AAA.

46. James Johnson Sweeney, *Stuart Davis* (New York: The Museum of Modern Art, 1945), p. 13. Davis worked for Walter Lippmann, who headed a special commission to prepare for a peace conference.

47. Phillips transcript, pp. 191–92.

48. Sweeney, *Stuart Davis*, p. 13, cites the end of 1918 (the year of the great flu epidemic) as the date when Davis got influenza; other scholars cite 1919, that is, just before he went to Cuba. See also Karen Wilkin, "Stuart Davis: The Cuban Watercolors," *Latin American Art* 2 (Spring 1990), pp. 29–43.

II. Modernist Experimentation: The 1920s

1. The classic study of the 1920s is Frederick Lewis Allen, *Only Yesterday: An Informal History of the 1920s* (1931; rpt. New York: Harper & Row, 1964).

2. See John R. Lane and Susan C. Larsen, *Abstract Painting and Sculpture in America, 1927–1944* (Pittsburgh: Museum of Art, Carnegie Institute, 1983), for a summary of arts organizations showing modernist work in the 1920s. See also Zilczer, "Modern Art and Its Sources: Exhibitions in New York, 1910–1925."

3. Modern Artists of America, Inc., "Exhibition by Members," Joseph Brummer Galleries, New York, April 1–30, 1922; Stuart Davis Papers, AAA. Only one woman, Marguerite Zorach, was included among the "younger men."

4. Quoted in Dickran Tashjian, *William Carlos Williams and the American Scene, 1920–1940* (New York: Whitney Museum of American Art, 1978), p. 62, from William Carlos Williams, *I Wanted to Write a Poem: The Autobiography of the Works of a Poet*, ed. Edith Heal (Boston: Beacon Press, 1958), p. 29.

5. Quoted in Tashjian, *William*

Carlos Williams, p. 62.

6. The original journal, called Notebook 1920–22, belongs to a dealer in New Mexico. A poor-quality microfilm is in the Stuart Davis Papers, AAA, Roll 3842.

7. See the Introduction, above, note 9.

8. Davis, "The Universal Figuring Book," May 1920, pp. 3, 7, in Notebook 1920–22; Stuart Davis Papers, AAA, Roll 3842.

9. Ibid., p. 3.

10. Ibid., p. 10.

11. For a reproduction of the notebook page that includes this quotation, see Lewis Kachur, "Stuart Davis's Word-Pictures," in Sims, *Stuart Davis, American Painter,* p. 99. Later, Davis would disparage illustration.

12. Henry McBride, "Whitney Studio Club Opens an Exhibition," *New York Sunday Herald,* May 8, 1921; Stuart Davis Papers (Scrapbook), AAA.

13. Rudi Blesh, *Modern Art U.S.A.: Men, Rebellion, Conquest, 1900–1956* (New York: Knopf, 1956), p. 96.

14. Konrad Cramer's untitled 1921 collage (Weatherspoon Art Gallery, University of North Carolina at Greensboro) is rather close to some of Davis's work in its wit, style, and technique; Barbara Zabel, in "The Avant-Garde Automaton: Two Collages by Stuart Davis," *Archives of American Art Journal* 32, no. 1 (1992), pp. 11–15, relates *ITLKSEZ* (plate 41) and Davis's untitled work (plate 40) to the spirit of Man Ray's Dada-influenced machine imagery. Zabel has, moreover, astutely observed that the black, masklike face of *ITLK-SEZ* "inevitably evokes African sculpture and primitivism" (p. 15).

15. Barbara Zabel, "Stuart Davis's Appropriation of Advertising: The Tobacco Series, 1921–1924," *American Art* 5 (Fall 1991), pp. 57–67.

16. Davis, Notebook 1920–22, Stuart Davis Papers, AAA: February 1922, p. 69, and May 29, 1921, p. 39; quoted in Zabel, "Stuart Davis's Appropriation of Advertising," p. 58. Margo S. Ballantyne, in "The Effect of Advertising in the Early Works of Stuart Davis" (M.A. thesis, University of Oregon, 1991), offers original analyses of both the early 1920s collages with the Tobacco Cubist compositions.

17. Neil Harris, "Designers on Demand: Art and the Modern Corporation," in *Art, Design, and the Modern Corporation* (Washington, D.C.: National Museum of American Art and the Smithsonian Institution Press, 1985), pp. 12, 25, note 22. The other jurors also included the muralist Edwin H. Blashfield, the illustrator Charles Dana Gibson, the etcher Joseph Pennell, and the art educator Arthur W. Dowe.

18. Quoted in Zabel, "Stuart Davis's Appropriation of Advertising," p. 60.

19. Davis, Notebook 1920–22, p. 113; Stuart Davis Papers, AAA. Also quoted in Ballantyne, "The Effect of Advertising in the Early Works of Stuart Davis," p. 32, note 41.

20. Audrey Flack recalls her student years at Yale when Davis was a visiting instructor, and being distracted during Davis's critiques of students' work by the growing length of the ash at the tip of Davis's cigarette.

21. Frank Stella, *Working Space: The Charles Eliot Norton Lectures, 1983–84* (Cambridge, Mass.: Harvard University Press, 1986), p. 5, succinctly states the modernist credo: "[T]he aim of art is to create space—space that is not compromised by decoration or illustration, space in which the subjects of painting can live."

22. Fogg Papers, Reel 1, "1923 (?)(b) no date"; Fogg.

23. See William C. Agee, *Stuart Davis (1892–1964): The Breakthrough Years, 1922–24* (New York: Salander-O'Reilly Galleries, 1987).

24. Walter Pach reviewed the show in the March 1920 issue of *The Dial.*

25. Quoted in Sweeney, *Stuart Davis,* p. 150.

26. Theresa Bernstein Meyerowitz, *William Meyerowitz: The Artist Speaks* (Cranbury, N.J.: Associated University Presses, 1986), p. 39.

27. *Gloucester Daily Times,* August 7, 1922. Quoted in James F. O'Gorman, "Parnassas on Ledge Road: The Life and Times of East Gloucester's Gallery-on-the-Moors, 1916–1922," in Crews, *The Red Cottage,* n.p.

28. *New York Evening Sun,* October 30, 1926; Stuart Davis Papers (Scrapbook), AAA.

29. Davis, "Recollections of the Whitney," p. 3.

30. "Stuart Davis," *New York Evening Post,* December 18, 1926, and undated, unidentified clipping of about the same date; Stuart Davis Papers (Scrapbook), AAA.

31. Davis, "Recollections of the Whitney," p. 4.

32. See Jane Heap, ed., "Machine-Age Exposition Catalogue," *The Little Review* 12, no. 1, Supplement (May 1927).

33. "Varied Attractions in Local Galleries," clipping inscribed "N.Y. Sun/Feb."; Stuart Davis Papers (Scrapbook), AAA.

34. Clipping inscribed "N.Y. Times/Dec. 4, 1927"; Stuart Davis Papers (Scrapbook), AAA.

35. Sweeney, *Stuart Davis,* p. 16–17.

36. "Stuart Davis and Glenn Coleman Together," *New York Sun,* inscribed "April 1928"; Stuart Davis Papers (Scrapbook), AAA.

37. Davis, "Recollections of the Whitney," p. 4. Details of the financial arrangements can be gleaned from WMAA.

38. Stuart Davis, "Self-Interview," *Creative Art* 9 (September 1931), p. 211. To Davis, the artists then representing the "American spirit" were Thomas Hart Benton, John Graham, Arshile Gorky, Paul Gaulois, Glenn O. Coleman, and Jan Matulka.

39. Davis, *Stuart Davis,* pp. [20, 22].

40. See Lewis Kachur, *Stuart Davis: An American in Paris* (New York: Whitney Museum of American Art, 1987).

41. Davis, *Stuart Davis,* p. [22].

42. Phillips transcript, pp. 299–300.

43. Elizabeth Hutton Turner, *American Artists in Paris, 1919–1929* (Ann Arbor: UMI Research Press, 1988), p. 39, note 74. See also Theresa Leininger-Miller's "African-American Artists in Paris, 1922–1934" (Ph.D. dissertation, Yale University, 1995).

44. Davis to his father, September 17, 1928; collection Earl Davis.

45. Ibid.

46. Davis to his mother, postcard of November 5, 1928; collection Earl Davis.

47. See Dougald McMillan, *transition: The History of a Literary Era, 1927–1938* (London: Calder & Boyars, 1975).

48. Elliot Paul, "Stuart Davis, American Painter," *transition* 14 (Fall 1928), pp. 146–47. On page 148, Paul writes: "Several young men gathered around him in the beginning and one by one have reverted to magazine cover decoration or three cheers for the soviets."

49. Davis to his mother, January 25, 1929; collection Earl Davis.

50. Phillips transcript, p. 58.

51. Quoted in Ione Robinson, *A Wall to Paint on* (New York: Dutton, 1946), pp. 45–46, 252. I am grateful to Tom Wolfe for this reference.

52. Quoted in Sweeney, *Stuart Davis,* p. 20.

53. I want to thank Wanda Corn for urging me to think about the role the calligraphic line played in these Paris scenes.

54. Sweeney, *Stuart Davis,* p. 21: "The very thing that made it interesting to me—the slowed-down tempo—made it monotonous. Having been born over here [the U.S.A.], with all this going on around you, you have a need for it. I didn't do anything there but paint and walk around the streets."

III. Political Protest and Social Theories of Art: The 1930s

1. Phillips transcript, pp. 177–78. Little is known of Bessie Chosak.

2. Notes of Stuart Davis's conversation with Hermon More and Baur on September 29, 1953; WMAA. In November 1928, Force and Whitney phased out the Whitney Studio Club and organized the Whitney Studio Galleries, which was run as a commer-

cial gallery to help the sales of contemporary art; see Tarbell, "Gertrude Vanderbilt Whitney as Patron," in Hills and Tarbell, *The Figurative Tradition and the Whitney Museum of American Art,* p. 16.

3. Lloyd Goodrich, "In the Galleries," *The Arts* 16 (February 1930), p. 432.

4. Quoted in "The New York Season," *The Art Digest* 4 (February 1, 1930), p. 17.

5. See the Introduction, above, for the continuation of Davis's thoughts on being Rembrandt-American.

6. Arshile Gorky to Duncan Phillips, February 3, 1930 [?]. In a letter of December 28 [n.d.], Graham writes to Phillips: "Stuart Davis, Gorky and myself have formed a group and something original, purely American is coming out from under our brushes." Both letters in the Phillips Collection Archives, Washington, D.C.; the second letter is quoted in Lewis Kachur, "Stuart Davis's Word-Pictures," in Sims, *Stuart Davis,* p. 108. Phillips bought his first Davis painting, *Blue Café,* in November 1930 for 300 dollars.

7. Discussed in Stuart Davis, "Arshile Gorky in the 1930's: A Personal Recollection," *Magazine of Art* 44 (February 1951), pp. 56–58; reprinted in Kelder, *Stuart Davis,* pp. 178–83.

8. Jacob Kainen, "Memories of Arshile Gorky," *Arts Magazine* 50 (March 1976), p. 96.

9. Stuart Davis, Introduction to *Recent Painting in Oil and Water Color by Stuart Davis* (New York: Downtown Gallery, 1931), n.p.; in Kelder, *Stuart Davis,* p. 111.

10. Edward Alden Jewell, in the *New York Times,* March 10, 1932; Stuart Davis Papers (Scrapbook), AAA.

11. Lincoln Kirstein to Stuart Davis, February 6, 1932; carbon copy of letter in the Archives of the Museum of Modern Art, New York. Kirstein asked if expenses would affect Davis's decision to participate; Davis replied on February 10 that his "participation would be greatly facilitated if the cost of the

materials was attended to by the Museum." On February 19, he wrote again and enclosed bills in the amount of $28.99. Most artists were not reimbursed.

12. The files of the Museum of Modern Art reveal that Alfred Barr worked tirelessly to prevent cancellation. The exhibition, however, was moved to a location in the museum that was virtually inaccessible to the public.

13. Malcolm Vaughan, "Modern Art Mural Exhibit A Sorry Show," *New York American,* May 7, 1932; AAA. For an analysis of the painting, see Bruce Weber, *Stuart Davis' New York* (West Palm Beach, Fla.: Norton Gallery and School of Art, 1985), pp. 12–16.

14. She had been living at 127 East Thirty-fifth Street, while he was living at 166 Second Avenue. Moreover, she died at a hospital in Brooklyn, the borough where her parents lived; their names are listed on the death certificate, whereas Davis's name is not, although her marital status at death is listed as "married."

15. "Largest Mural Work Ever Finished Here Goes to 'Roxy's' N.Y.," *Gloucester Daily Times,* November 12, 1932; Stuart Davis Papers (Scrapbook), AAA.

16. Sims, *Stuart Davis, American Painter,* p. 220.

17. According to Helen Farr Sloan, whose job it was to fire Davis, the artist then had only two students; conversation with the author, September 21, 1993.

18. Edith Halpert to Davis, contract dated October 1, 1930, and letter dated September 14, 1932; Edith Halpert Papers, AAA.

19. Diane Tepfer, "Edith Gregor Halpert and the Downtown Gallery, 1926–1940: A Study in American Art Patronage" (Ph.D. dissertation, University of Michigan, 1989), pp. 84–85.

20. "Good Barter," *The Art Digest* 6 (May 1, 1932), p. 7.

21. Such news items were quoted in *The Art Digest* 6 (June 1, 1932), p. 2.

22. *The Art Digest* 6 (July 1, 1932), p. 3; *The Art Digest* 6

(May 15, 1932), p. 17.

23. Stuart Davis to Edith Halpert, October 5, 1932; Edith Halpert Papers, AAA.

24. See Kachur, in Sims, *Stuart Davis, American Artist,* pp. 227–28, for a discussion of the painting

25. Phillips transcript, pp. 179–83.

26. Stuart Davis to Edith Halpert, September 29, 1933; Edith Halpert Papers, AAA.

27. Phillips transcript, pp. 181, 185–86.

28. For further information on the projects, see Francis V. O'Connor, ed., *The New Deal Art Projects: An Anthology of Memoirs* (Washington, D.C.: Smithsonian Institution Press, 1972).

29. Noted in Garnett McCoy "The Rise and Fall of the American Artists Congress," *Prospects* 13 (1982), p. 328.

30. The half-finished mural was stopped by Rockefeller's managers in May 1933. Diego Rivera was paid money owed and the mural was covered. The final destruction occurred one night in February 1934. See Lucienne Bloch, "On Location with Diego Rivera," *Art in America* 74 (February 1986), pp. 102–23.

31. When retail employees went on strike at the Ohrbach's Department Store in February 1935, the Artists Union joined in their protests; Davis, along with other militants, was arrested for his efforts. See the newspaper clipping headed "Thirty-one Face Court for Picketing at Ohrbach's," *Daily Worker,* February 4, 1935; Stuart Davis Papers (Scrapbook), AAA.

32. *New York Sun,* April 28, 1934; Stuart Davis Papers (Scrapbook), AAA.

33. Phillips transcript, pp. 282–83.

34. The break is charted in the Edith Halpert Papers, AAA.

35. Phillips transcript, p. 333; passage quoted in "An Interview with Stuart Davis," *Archives of American Art Journal* 31 (1991), p. 11.

36. See the Minutes of the Editorial Board, January 22, 1936; Stuart Davis Papers (Restricted), AAA.

37. See Patricia Hills, "1936: Meyer Schapiro, *Art Front,*

and the Popular Front," *Oxford Art Journal* 17, no. 1 (1994), pp. 30–40.

38. Stuart Davis, "Paintings by Salvador Dali," *Art Front* 1 (January 1935), p. 7; Clarence Weinstock, "Letter on Salvador Dali," *Art Front* 1 (February 1935), p. 8. Davis later called Dali a fascist; Fogg Papers, Reel 4 (January 16, 1942[b]), p. 1.

39. *Time,* December 24, 1934.

40. Stuart Davis, "The New York American Scene in Art," *Art Front* 1 (February 1935), p. 61; reprinted in Kelder, ed., *Stuart Davis,* pp. 151–54.

41. Stuart Davis, Introduction to *Abstract Painting in America* (New York: Whitney Museum of American Art, 1935); in Kelder, *Stuart Davis,* p. 113.

42. Clarence Weinstock, "Contradictions and Abstrations," *Art Front* 1 (April 1935), p. 7.

43. Stuart Davis, "A Medium of Two Dimensions," *Art Front* 1 (May 1935), p. 6; in Kelder, *Stuart Davis,* pp. 114–16. Anita Duquette of the Whitney Museum staff, in a letter to the author of July 6, 1992, confirmed that Davis had one and a half pages cut from his essay.

44. Fogg Papers, October 1, 1935.

45. Davis seems to have been reacting to Schapiro's "Social Bases of Art," delivered to the American Artists Congress in February 1936 and later published as part of the papers of the AAC. In the entry dated January 20, 1937, Davis criticized many approaches, including Schapiro's.

46. See the papers published in *First American Artists Congress* (New York: American Artists Congress, 1936); reprinted in Matthew Baigell and Julia Williams, eds., *Artists Against War and Fascism: Papers of the First American Artists Congress* (New Brunswick, N.J.: Rutgers University Press, 1986). See also the Stuart Davis Papers (Restricted), AAA. I am grateful to Earl Davis for permission to read the files.

47. Phillips transcript, p. 188–89.

48. Holger Cahill, *New Horizons in American Art* (New York: The Museum of Modern Art, 1936), p. 18.

49. Burgoyne Diller, "Abstract Murals," in Francis V. O'Connor, ed., *Art for the Millions: Essays from the 1930s by Artists and Administrators of the W.P.A. Federal Art Project* (Boston: New York Graphic Society, 1973), p. 69.

50. Stuart Davis Papers (Restricted), AAA.

51. I want to thank Earl Davis for providing this information.

52. For the shifts in the Communist Party line on the war in Europe, see the issues of the *New Masses* from September through December 1939.

53. See Garnett McCoy, "The Rise and Fall of the American Artists Congress," *Prospects* 13 (1988), pp. 325–40.

IV. Hot and Cool Abstraction: The 1940s to the 1960s

1. Stuart Davis, "The Cube Root," *Art News* 41 (February 1, 1943), p. 34; in Kelder, *Stuart Davis*, pp. 130–31.

2. Stuart Davis to Juliana Force, September 13, 1939, and Juliana Force to Stuart Davis, October 10, 1939; WMAA. Stuart Davis to Duncan Phillips, September 15, 1939; Stuart Davis to Duncan Phillips, December 15, 1939; Stuart Davis to Elmira Bier, March 20, 1940; Duncan Phillips to Stuart Davis, October 17, 1939, and March 23, 1940; Archives of the Phillips Collection, Washington, D.C.

3. Phillips transcript, p. 383.

4. Stuart Davis to Juliana Force, March 22, 1940; WMAA. He also tried to sell the book idea to Samuel Golden of the American Artists Group in early 1940; see American Artists Group Papers, AAA.

5. Stuart Davis to Juliana Force, October 29, 1940, and January 18, 1941; Juliana Force to Stuart Davis, November 1, 1940; WMAA. I am grateful to Nancy Roden for providing the purchase-price figures. According to U.S. Department of Commerce statistics (1971), in 1940 it took the average college teacher about two months to earn 500 dollars; see *Historical Statistics of the United States, Colonial Times to 1970*, Part 1 (Washington, D.C.: U.S. Gov-

ernment Printing Office, 1975), p. 176.

6. Stuart Davis to Mrs. [Elizabeth] Sharkey, July 14, 1941; WMAA. Just four days later, on July 18, 1941, Davis swallowed his pride and wrote to Halpert to ask whether she would again be his dealer; Edith Halpert Papers, AAA.

7. Olin Dows to Solomon R. Guggenheim, July 19, 1941; WMAA.

8. See the references to Hammond in Eileen Southern, *The Music of Black Americans: A History* (New York: Norton, 1971).

9. Phillips transcript, p. 300–4.

10. I am grateful to Earl Davis for sending me transcripts of the daily calendars.

11. Quoted in Earl Davis, *The Fine Art of Jazz* (New York: The Jazz Foundation of America, 1991), n.p.

12. Quoted in Mona Hadler, "Jazz and the Visual Arts," *Arts Magazine* 57 (June 1983), p. 98, citing Albert Murray, "The Visual Equivalent of the Blues," *Romare Bearden: 1970–1980* (Charlotte, N.C.: Mint Museum, 1980), pp. 17–28.

13. Fogg Papers, January 18, 1942. In this same entry, Davis wrote: "Louis Armstrong plays many popular tunes of the most inane and sentimental kind, 'Sweethearts on Parade' for example. But he starts right off with a severe architecture of rhythms that completely changes the intent of the song writer. He even sings the silly lyrics, but here again he interpolates new words, leaves out other[s], and the silly lyric becomes real poetry. Disney, on the other hand, can take great music like the 'Sacre du Printemps' and reduce it to the level of a banal illustration."

14. Babette Edelston, "A Fond Remembrance: A Former Student Recalls How His Class Was Conducted, How He Taught and What She Learned"; manuscript in WMAA.

15. Naomi Miller, conversation with the author, September 24, 1993.

16. Fogg Papers, January 7, 1942.

17. Fogg Papers, January 19, 1942 (b), pp. 5–6.

18. Lane, *Stuart Davis*, pp. 55–64.

19. Fogg Papers, March 1942, Index, p. 1.

20. Fogg Papers, March 28, 1942, Index, p. 1.

21. Edward Alden Jewell, "Downtown Holds Fall Art Display," *New York Times*, September 22, 1942, p. 24; Stuart Davis, *New York Times*, September 27, 1942.

22. Rudi Blesh, *Stuart Davis* (New York: Grove Press, 1960), p. 58.

23. Sims, *Stuart Davis, American Painter*, p. 261.

24. Blesh, *Stuart Davis*, p. 58.

25. Phillips transcript, p. 302.

26. Stuart Davis, "Memo on Mondrian," *Arts Magazine Yearbook* (1961); in Kelder, *Stuart Davis*, p. 186.

27. Ibid.

28. See, for example, Fogg Papers, January 1942.

29. All quoted in Peyton Boswell, "Painted Jazz," *The Art Digest* 17 (February 15, 1943), p. 3.

30. Robert M. Coates, "The Art Galleries," *The New Yorker* 18 (February 13, 1943), p. 58; Clement Greenberg, "Stuart Davis," *The Nation* 156 (February 20, 1943), p. 284.

31. Alfred H. Barr, Jr., *What Is Modern Painting?* (New York: The Museum of Modern Art, 1943), p. 4.

32. Holger Cahill, "Stuart Davis in Retrospect, 1945–1910," *Art News* 44 (October 15–31, 1945), p. 24.

33. *New Masses*, November 27, 1945; in Kelder, *Stuart Davis*, p. 196.

34. See Tepfer, "Edith Gregor Halpert and the Downtown Gallery," p. 253.

35. See "Stuart Davis/Owners," transcript dated January 1946; WMAA.

36. Winthrop Sargeant, "Why Artists Are Going Abstract: The Case of Stuart Davis," *Life* 22 (February 17, 1947), pp. 78–83.

37. See *Congressional Record*, May 13, 1947, p. 5222. He was one of the artists selected for the "Advancing American Art" exhibition of 1946—subsequently canceled when the press began red-baiting it for its inclusion of radical artists.

38. Clement Greenberg, *Art and*

Culture: Critical Essays (Boston: Beacon Press, 1961), p. 211.

39. John I. H. Baur, *Revolution and Tradition in Modern American Art* (New York: Praeger, 1951), pp. 64, 69.

40. Phillips transcript, p. 88.

41. Fogg Papers, September 20, 1948, p. 1.

42. Ibid.

43. Stuart Davis, "Mural, *Allée*, for Drake University" (1955), in Kelder, *Stuart Davis*, p. 94.

44. Dorothy Gees Seckler, "Stuart Davis Paints a Picture," *Art News* 52 (June–August 1953), p. 31.

45. Other couplings include the following: *Tournos* of 1954 (Munson - Williams - Proctor Institute, Utica, New York) and *Memo* of 1956 (National Museum of American Art, Smithsonian Institution, Washington, D.C.) were based on *Shapes of Landscape Space* of 1939 (The Neuberger Museum, State University of New York, Purchase); *Medium Still Life* of 1953 (William H. Lane Collection) and *Something on the Eight Ball* of 1953–54 (Philadelphia Museum of Art) were based on *Matches* of 1927 (The Chrysler Museum, Norfolk, Virginia); and *Colonial Cubism* of 1954 (Walker Art Center, Minneapolis) and *Memo No. 2* of 1956 (Southwestern Bell Corporation Collection, St. Louis) were both based on Davis's small oil on canvas *Landscape, Gloucester* of 1922 (collection John F. Lott, Lubbock, Texas).

46. See *American Artist* 28 (December 1964), p. 8.

47. E. C. Goossen, *Stuart Davis* (New York: George Braziller, 1959), p. 12.

48. Donald Judd, "In the Galleries: Stuart Davis," *Arts Magazine* 36 (September 1962), p. 44.

49. See Brian O'Doherty, "Stuart Davis: A Memoir," *Evergreen Review* 10 (February 1966), p. 24.

50. Brian O'Doherty, "Davis's Work Was Never Out of Date—He Anticipated Movements in Art," *New York Times*, June 26, 1964, p. 26.

51. Will Barnet, interview with the author, November 17, 1992.

Chronology

1892   December 7: Born Edward Stuart Davis in Philadelphia to Helen Stuart Foulke Davis, a sculptor, and Edward Wyatt Davis, art editor for the *Philadelphia Press*.

1901   Family moves to East Orange, New Jersey, when Edward Davis takes a job at the *Newark Evening News*.

1906   February 14: Birth of only brother, Wyatt Davis.

1909   Fall: Attends Robert Henri's art school at 1947 Broadway in Manhattan. Becomes friends with Glenn Coleman and Henry Glintenkamp.

1910   April: Encouraged by Henri and by John Sloan, participates in the "Exhibition of Independent Artists," showing five oil paintings.

1912   With Glintenkamp, rents studio space in the Terminal Building on Hudson Street in Hoboken, New Jersey.

1913   February–March: Shows five watercolors in the "International Exhibition of Modern Art" (the Armory Show) at the Sixty-ninth Regiment Armory; the exhibition includes some 1,300 works.
        Submits drawings to the socialist magazine *The Masses* and to *Harper's Weekly*.
        Summer: Is in Provincetown, Massachusetts, a flourishing art colony.
        Fall: Moves with Glintenkamp to a studio in the Lincoln Arcade, at 1931 Broadway, New York; Coleman joins them. Is included in a group exhibition at the MacDowell Club, New York.

1914   Summer: Returns to Provincetown; meets Charles Demuth.

1915   Summer: Visits the Sloans and other *Masses* staff artists in Gloucester, Massachusetts. Continues to summer there until 1934.

1916   With Sloan, Coleman, and four other artists resigns from the staff of *The Masses* in a policy dispute.
        September: Submits paintings to the inaugural exhibition, devoted to Gloucester artists, of the Gallery-on-the-Moors, Gloucester, Massachusetts.

1917   December: First solo exhibition (watercolors and drawings), Sheridan Square Gallery, New York.

1918   Works as a cartographer for U.S. Army Intelligence.
        February: Participates in "Exhibition of Indigenous Painting," Whitney Studio Club, New York.
        Spring: Shows at the Ardsley Gallery, Brooklyn.
        Begins to write about his art theories.

1919   Summer: Visits Tioga, Pennsylvania, before going on to Gloucester.
        December: Travels with Coleman to Cuba.

1920   August: Has four drawings published in the avant-garde literary magazine *The Dial;* will continue submitting drawings to the magazine until 1923.
        The poet William Carlos Williams selects one of the Gloucester drawings as the frontispiece for his volume *Kora in Hell: Improvisations*.

1921   April: Along with Joaquín Torres-García and Stanislaw Szukalski, has an exhibition at the Whitney Studio Club.

1922   Joins the Modern Artists of America and exhibits with them at the Joseph Brummer Galleries, New York. With friends, organizes the Gloucester Society of Arts—an alternative to the conservative North Shore Arts Association—and becomes chairman.

1923   Summer: Drives to Santa Fe, New Mexico, with the Sloans and his brother, Wyatt.

1925   February: First solo museum exhibition, the Newark Museum, New Jersey.

1926   October: Group exhibition at the Charles Daniel Gallery, New York.
        December: Retrospective exhibition of forty-three paintings at the Whitney Studio Club, New York; five works are sold from the show. Gertrude Vanderbilt Whitney begins providing a monthly allowance of 125 dollars, an arrangement that lasts for a year.

1927   November–December: Having joined the Downtown Gallery, New York, directed by Edith Halpert, has first exhibition there. Begins the Egg Beater series.

1928   April–May: The four Egg Beater paintings are included in an exhibition with Glenn Coleman at the Valentine Gallery, New York.

May: Participates in an exhibition of flower paintings at the Downtown Gallery, New York.

Summer: Juliana Force, acting for Mrs. Whitney, gives him 900 dollars so that he can go to Paris. There rents the former apartment of Jan Matulka; meets Fernand Léger, Gertrude Stein, and American expatriate painters living in the Montparnasse district.

Fall: An article on his work, by Elliot Paul, is published in the magazine *transition*, based in Paris.

Late in the year or early in 1929: In Paris, marries Bessie Chosak, from Brooklyn.

1929   Summer: Returns with Bessie to New York. Goes on to Gloucester for the late summer months.

November–December: Small exhibition of watercolors at the Whitney Studio Galleries, New York.

Winter: His Paris lithographs are included in the Downtown Gallery's Christmastime exhibition of American prints.

1930   January: Solo exhibition at Edith Halpert's Downtown Gallery, New York.

February: Defends his views on art in the periodical *Creative Art.*

October: Edith Halpert begins sending him a monthly stipend in exchange for his painting output.

December: Included in the Museum of Modern Art's second show of contemporary art, "Painting and Sculpture by Living Americans."

1931   April: Exhibits the works known as New York/Paris series at the Downtown Gallery, New York; for the catalogue writes a lengthy essay on his personal art theories.

1932   Spring: Teaches at the Art Students League of New York.

March: Solo exhibition at the Downtown Gallery, New York, featuring new work.

May: Included in a controversial exhibition of mural designs held at the Museum of Modern Art, New York.

Summer: Secures a commission from the interior designer Donald Deskey to paint a mural for the Men's Lounge at Radio City Music Hall, New York.

June 15: Bessie Chosak Davis dies.

Monthly stipend from Halpert becomes increasingly irregular due to the depressed art market.

December: Included in the first Biennial exhibition of the Whitney Museum of American Art, New York.

1933   Spring: Teaches in his own rooms but by summer has to abandon his place for lack of funds.

September: Halpert writes that she can no longer afford to give him a monthly allowance. Spends most of the remainder of the year in Gloucester.

Christmas: Returns to New York; moves in with his brother Wyatt.

Late December: Finds employment with the Public Works of Art program, set up by the Treasury Section to employ artists to make public art, and joins the radical John Reed Club.

1934   Joins the Artists Union, a trade union set up for artists that year. Moves to 43 Seventh Avenue.

December: Becomes editor-in-chief of *Art Front*, the monthly magazine of the Artists Union.

1935   February–March: Shows work in the exhibition "Abstract American Painting" at the Whitney Museum of American Art, New York, and writes an introduction for the catalogue. Becomes more critical of the gallery and private patronage system and has a falling out with Edith Halpert and the Downtown Gallery.

Summer: Meets with Alexander Trachtenberg and others to set up the American Artists Congress.

August: Joins the Federal Art Project, which, under the aegis of the Works Progress Administration, assists needy artists.

1936   January: Leaves the staff of *Art Front.*

February: The American Artists Congress meets for three days at Town Hall and the New School for Social Research. He will steer the organization for the next four years, first as its executive secretary and then as national chairman.

March: Severs ties with the Downtown Gallery.

1937	Under the auspices of the W.P.A. paints *Swing Landscape* for the Williamsburg Housing Project, Brooklyn, New York, but the work is never installed there.
	December: The American Artists Congress holds its second large conference.
1938	February 25: Marries Roselle Springer.
1939	Hired by Donald Deskey to paint a mural, *The History of Communications,* for the New York World's Fair. Forced off the Federal Art Project by new rules restricting length of employment.
1940	April: Resigns from the American Artists Congress. By now soured on radical politics, will devote the rest of his life to his own art. Will make greater effort to sell his work to museums, with mixed results.
	Begins teaching at the New School for Social Research (through 1950). Increasingly is associated with jazz musicians.
1941	July: Writes to Edith Halpert, asking her to take him back into the Downtown Gallery. She agrees.
	Exhibits with Marsden Hartley at the Cincinnati Modern Art Society.
1942	Receives a commission for a rug from the Museum of Modern Art, New York.
	December: Included in the exhibition "Artists for Victory" at the Metropolitan Museum of Art, New York.
1943	February: Has his first solo exhibition at the Downtown Gallery since 1934; jazz musician friends perform at the opening.
1944	Wins first prize for *The Terminal* (1937) at Pepsi-Cola's "Portrait of America" exhibition.
1945	October: Retrospective exhibition at the Museum of Modern Art, New York, organized by James Johnson Sweeney.
	Autobiography is published in the monograph series of American Artists Group.
1946	Included in the controversial exhibition "Advancing American Art," circulated by the United States Information Agency throughout the U.S. until its cancellation.
1948	Named one of the ten best painters in America in a poll of critics and museum directors, conducted by *Look* magazine. Until the end of his lifetime, will regularly receive prizes and awards from museums and art organizations.
1951	Teaches at the Yale University Art School.
	October: Work is included in the first Bienal de São Paulo, Brazil.
1952	Receives a John Simon Guggenheim Memorial Foundation fellowship.
	April 17: Son, George Earl Davis, is born.
	June: Solo exhibition in the U.S. pavilion at the Venice Biennale.
1955	Commissioned to design a mural for Drake University in Des Moines, Iowa.
	Moves to 15 West Sixty-seventh Street, New York.
1956	Elected to the National Institute of Arts and Letters. Is included in the American group exhibition at the Venice Biennale.
1957	Receives a commission to design a mural for the H. J. Heinz Research Center, Pittsburgh.
	March: Retrospective exhibition opens at the Walker Art Center, Minneapolis; exhibition travels to Des Moines, San Francisco, and New York.
1958	Wins the Solomon R. Guggenheim Museum International Award; wins the same award again in 1960.
1959	Included in "American Painting and Sculpture," a controversial exhibition organized by the United States Information Agency for travel to Moscow.
1962	April: Solo exhibition of paintings done from 1958 to 1962 held at the Downtown Gallery, New York.
1964	June 24: Dies of a stroke.

Selected Bibliography

The Bibliography includes a selection of books, catalogues, and essays about Davis's career and aspects of his oeuvre and about the context of twentieth-century American art within which he worked. Diane Kelder, ed., *Stuart Davis*, 1971, reprints many of Davis's own writings and unpublished journal entries. A complete bibliography for Davis is contained in Lowery Stokes Sims, *Stuart Davis: American Painter*, 1991.

Books and Major Catalogues

AGEE, WILLIAM C. *Stuart Davis: The Breakthrough Years.* New York: Salander-O'Reilly Galleries, 1987.

ARNASON, H. H. *Stuart Davis.* Minneapolis: Walker Art Center, 1957.

BAIGELL, MATTHEW, and JULIA WILLIAMS, eds. *Artists Against War and Fascism: Papers of the First American Artists Congress.* New Brunswick, N.J.: Rutgers University Press, 1986.

BAUR, JOHN I. H. *Revolution and Tradition in Modern American Art.* Cambridge, Mass.: Harvard University Press, 1951.

BLESH, RUDI. *Stuart Davis.* New York: Grove Press, 1960.

CREWS, BRITT. *The Red Cottage.* Gloucester, Mass.: Cape Ann Historical Association, 1992.

DAVIS, STUART. Autobiographical statement in *Stuart Davis.* New York: American Artists Group, 1945.

The Fiftieth Anniversary of the Exhibition of Independent Artists in 1910. Wilmington, Del.: Delaware Art Center, 1960.

GOOSSEN, E. C. *Stuart Davis.* New York: George Braziller, 1959.

KACHUR, LEWIS. *Stuart Davis: An American in Paris.* New York: Whitney Museum of American Art at Philip Morris, 1987.

KELDER, DIANE, ed. *Stuart Davis: A Documentary Monograph.* New York: Praeger, 1971.

LANE, JOHN R. *Stuart Davis: Art and Art Theory.* Brooklyn, N.Y.: The Brooklyn Museum, 1978.

LANE, JOHN R., and SUSAN C. LARSEN, eds. *Abstract Painting and Sculpture in America, 1927–1944.* Pittsburgh: Museum of Art, Carnegie Institute, in association with Harry N. Abrams, Inc., 1983.

MYERS, JANE, ed. *Stuart Davis: Graphic Work and Related Paintings with a Catalogue Raisonné of the Prints.* Essay by Diane Kelder. Catalogue Raisonné by Sylvan Cole and Jane Myers. Fort Worth: Amon Carter Museum, 1986.

O'DOHERTY, BRIAN. *American Masters: The Voice and the Myth.* New York: Random House, 1974.

POWELL, RICHARD J. *The Blues Aesthetic: Black Culture and Modernism.* Washington, D.C.: Washington Project for the Arts, 1989.

SIMS, LOWERY STOKES. *Stuart Davis: American Painter.* Essays by Sims, William C. Agee, Robert Hunter, Lewis Kachur, Diane Kelder, John R. Lane, and Karen Wilkin. New York: The Metropolitan Museum of Art, 1991. This recent major catalogue has a thorough bibliography.

SIMS, PATTERSON. *Stuart Davis: A Concentration of Works from the Permanent Collection of the Whitney Museum of American Art.* New York: Whitney Museum of American Art, 1980.

Stuart Davis: Retrospective, 1995. Essays by Earl Davis and Wayne Roosa; chronology by Patricia Hills. Tokyo: The Yomiuri Shimbun and the Japan Association of Art Museums, 1995.

SWEENEY, JAMES JOHNSON. *Stuart Davis.* New York: The Museum of Modern Art, 1945.

TASHJIAN, DICKRAN. *William Carlos Williams and the American Scene, 1920–1940.* New York: Whitney Museum of American Art, 1978.

TEPFER, DIANE. *Edith Gregor Halpert and the Downtown Gallery, 1926–1940: A Study in American Art Patronage.* Ann Arbor, Mich.: U.M.I. Research Press, 1989.

Turner, Elizabeth Hutton. *American Artists in Paris 1919–1929.* Ann Arbor, Mich.: U.M.I. Research Press, 1988.

Urdang, Beth. *Stuart Davis: Murals.* New York: Zabriskie Gallery, 1976.

Weber, Bruce. *Stuart Davis' New York.* West Palm Beach, Fla.: Norton Gallery and School of Art, 1985.

Whiting, Cécile. *Antifascism in American Art.* New Haven, Conn.: Yale University Press, 1989.

Wilkin, Karen. *Stuart Davis.* New York: Abbeville Press, 1987.

Wilken, Karen, and Lewis Kachur. *The Drawings of Stuart Davis: The Amazing Continuity.* New York: The American Federation of Arts in association with Harry N. Abrams, Inc., 1992.

Wilken, Karen, and Lori Potolsky. *Stuart Davis (1892–1964): Motifs and Versions.* New York: Salander-O'Reilly Galleries, 1988.

Wilson, William. *Stuart Davis's Abstract Argot.* San Francisco: Pomegranate Artbooks, 1993.

Zurier, Rebecca. *Art for "The Masses": A Radical Magazine and Its Graphics, 1911–1917.* Philadelphia: Temple University Press, 1988.

Essays and Articles

Davis, Earl. "Stuart Davis: Scapes, 1910–1923." In *Stuart Davis: Scapes—An Exhibition of Landscapes, Cityscapes and Seascapes Made between 1910 and 1923.* New York: Salander-O'Reilly Galleries, 1990.

———. "Stuart Davis: A Celebration in Jazz." In Earl Davis, ed., *The Fine Art of Jazz: A Stuart Davis Centennial Celebration.* New York: The Jazz Foundation of America, 1991.

Grad, Bonnie L. "Stuart Davis and Contemporary Culture." *Artibus et historiae,* no. 24 (1991), pp. 165–91.

Homer, William Innes. "Stuart Davis, 1894–1964: Last Interview." *Art News* 63 (September 1964), pp. 43, 56.

Kachur, Lewis. "Stuart Davis and Bob Brown: *The Masses* to *The Paris Bit.*" *Arts Magazine* 57 (October 1982), pp. 70–73.

———. "Stuart Davis: A Classicist Eclipsed." *Art International* 4 (Autumn 1988), pp. 17–21.

Kozloff, Max. "Larry Rivers, Stuart Davis and Slang Idiom." *Artforum* 4 (November 1965), pp. 20–24.

Lucas, John. "The Fine Art Jive of Stuart Davis." *Arts Magazine* 31 (September 1957), pp. 32–37.

McCoy, Garnett, ed. "An Interview with Stuart Davis." *Archives of American Art Journal* 31, no. 2 (1991), pp. 4–13.

O'Doherty, Brian. "Stuart Davis: A Memoir." *Evergreen Review* 10 (February 1966), pp. 22–27.

Seckler, Dorothy Gees. "Stuart Davis Paints a Picture." *Art News* 52 (June–August 1953), pp. 30–33, 74–75.

Wilkin, Karen. "Stuart Davis in His Own Time." *The New Criterion* 6 (January 1988), pp. 50–55.

———. "Stuart Davis: The Cuban Watercolors." *Latin American Art* 2 (Spring 1990), pp. 39–43.

Zabel, Barbara. "Stuart Davis's Appropriation of Advertising: *The Tobacco Series, 1921–1924.*" *American Art* 5 (Fall 1991), pp. 57–67.

———. "The Avant-Garde Automaton: Two Collages by Stuart Davis." *Archives of American Art Journal* 32, no. 1 (1992), pp. 11–15.

Photograph Credits